DISC
M
AND
MID WEST SCOTLAND

In the same series

DISCOVERING EDINBURGH

—

DISCOVERING GLASGOW

—

DISCOVERING ABERDEEN

DISCOVERING
MULL
AND
MID WEST SCOTLAND

P A MACNAB

RICHARD DREW PUBLISHING

FIRST PUBLISHED 1982

Published by
Richard Drew Publishing Ltd
20 Park Circus
Glasgow
G3 6BE

ISBN 0 904002 93 4

Made and printed in Great Britain by
William Collins Sons & Co. Ltd. Glasgow

Contents

Introduction

A GLANCE AT THE MAP WILL SHOW HOW the roads running north-west from Glasgow and the Lowlands converge naturally on Dalriada, the first and ancient kingdom of the invading Celtic Scots — Argyll. Oban, well-named in the past the 'Charing Cross of the Highlands' and 'Gateway to the Hebrides', together with Fort William, centre of the road system for the north and west, are the two main focal points. Argyll is a land of mighty mountains, lochs and glens, deeply-penetrated by the long wedge of the Firth of Lorne striking in from the Atlantic. It is a land of wide moorlands and far horizons, cairns and castles and ancient coastal forts; in places dotted with the deserted homes of once thriving communities replaced by sheep farms, which in turn became deer forests and sporting estates. It is a land still inhabited by their descendants, a kindly people whose history and traditions go back into pre-history.

Within the area lies the highest mountain in Britain; the longest loch; the deepest loch — and second deepest in Europe; the largest area of fresh water in Great Britain. Not the earliest, but the best-known introduction of Christianity came here in the year 563 with Columba and his disciples, to the little island of Iona off the south-west corner of Mull, regarded now as the most sacred island in the world.

West of Argyll and dominating the horizon lies the island famous in song and story as 'Mull of the Mountains'. Mull for music and story telling, unique among the Isles of the Hebrides for its variety of interests. A fascinating island that lays its spell on you, third largest of the Hebrides, described by Dugald MacPhail, the Mull Bard, as 'Of Isles the Fairest'. Lying as it does almost an extension of the mainland peninsula of Morvern, from which it is divided by the Sound of Mull, a channel only two miles wide at one point, it has close affinities with both the islands and the mainland, and of course it is readily accessible.

When describing the countryside it is difficult to decide what to present to readers. Do we appeal to the motorist who is studying his average speed between petrol stations; or the hiker, who loathes the main roads; or the mountaineer, who soars above the lot and seeks only to learn some new and exciting route to the tops — or the historian — the student — or just the man who likes to roam around and absorb the atmosphere?

In this book we shall tell you how to get to the area, and what you will see as you go along, both beside and off the roads. We shall tell you tales of the past, of clans and castles, stories about and by local worthies, and about the vanished race who raised the standing stones and fortified the coasts.

With the excellent local advice and service

obtainable at such modern information centres as those in Oban and Fort William it would be tedious to involve readers in too much local detail, which in any case would be incomplete. Sometimes a round at the village inn in the evening can yield far more information than a day's round of the countryside. Our aim is to use the brush rather than the pencil: to present the background story of Mull and Mid West Scotland.

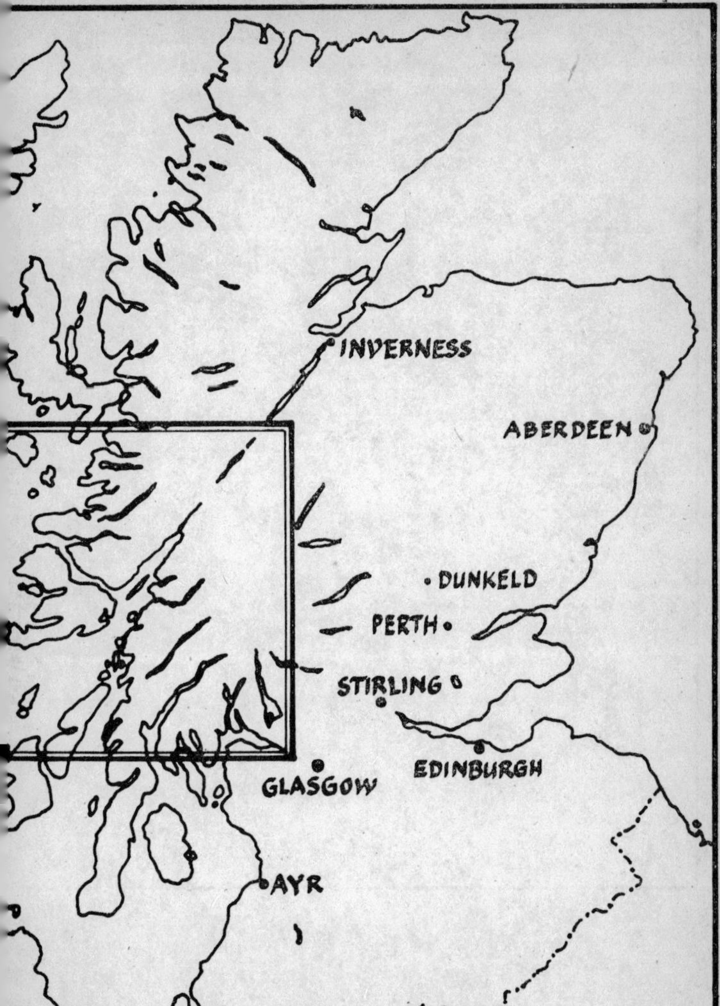
INVERNESS
ABERDEEN
DUNKELD
PERTH
STIRLING
EDINBURGH
GLASGOW
AYR

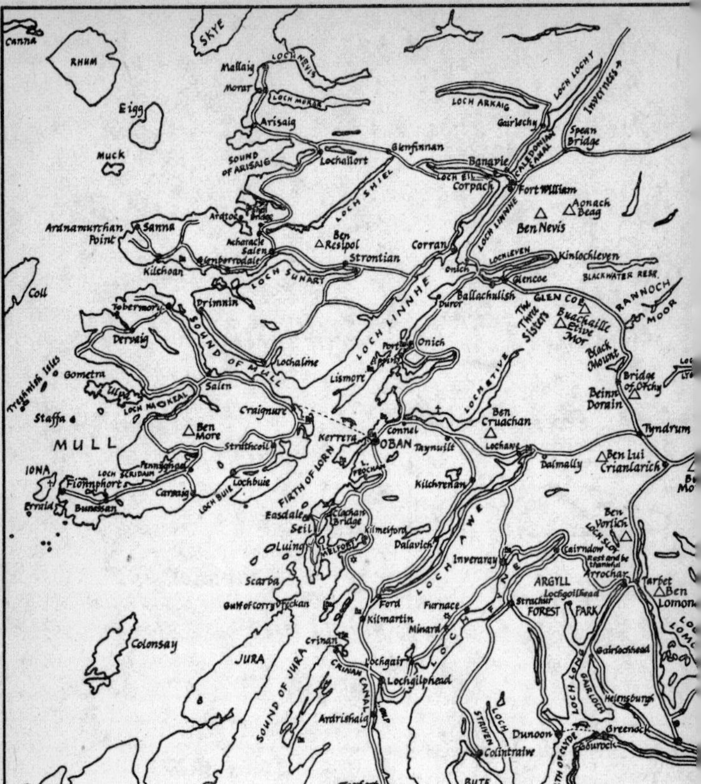

Canna
Rhum
Skye
Eigg
Muck
Mallaig
Loch Nevis
Morar
Loch Morar
Arisaig
Sound of Arisaig
Lochailort
Glenfinnan
Loch Shiel
Loch Arkaig
Gairlochy
Loch Lochy
Inverness
Spean Bridge
Caledonian Canal
Banavie
Loch Eil
Corpach
Fort William
Aonach Beag
Ben Nevis
Loch Linnhe
Ardnamurchan Point
Sanna
Acharacle
Salen
Ben Resipol
Strontian
Corran
Kilchoan
Glenborrodale
Loch Sunart
Lochleven
Kinlochleven
Blackwater Resr.
Onich
Glencoe
Coll
Tobermory
Drimnin
Ballachulish
Duror
Glen Coe
Rannoch
Moor
The Three Sisters
Buachaille Etive Mor
Dervaig
Sound of Mull
Onich
Port Appin
Lochaline
Black Mount
Treshnish Isles
Gometra
Ulva
Salen
Lismore
Loch Etive
Bridge of Orchy
Loch Na Keal
Craignure
Beinn Dorain
Staffa
Ben More
Ben Cruachan
Tyndrum
Mull
Kerrera
Connel
Oban
Taynuilt
Strathcoil
Lochawe
Iona
Loch Scridain
Dalmally
Ben Lui
Crianlarich
Pennyghael
Fionnphort
Lochbuie
Loch Buie
Carsaig
Firth of Lorn
Kilchrenan
Erraid
Bunessan
Easdale
Clachan Bridge
Seil
Kilmelford
Ben Vorlich
Loch Sloy
Dalavich
Luing
Melfort
Loch Awe
Inveraray
Cairndow
Rest and be thankful
Arrochar
Tarbet
Scarba
Argyll
Lochgoilhead
Ben Lomond
Ford
Furnace
Strachur
Forest
Park
Kilmartin
Minard
Colonsay
Crinan
Jura
Loch Fyne
Gairlochhead
Lochgair
Sound of Jura
Crinan Canal
Lochgilphead
Helensburgh
Loch Long
Gair Loch
Ardrishaig
Loch Striven
Dunoon
Greenock
Gourock
Colintraive
Firth of Clyde
Tarbert
Bute
Islay

Describing Mull and Mid West Scotland

THE NAME 'ARGYLL' MEANS THE LAND of the Strangers, the strangers being the Celtic race later called the Scots who came over from Ireland and founded the ancient kingdom of Dalriada, from which the lands of the Picts were infiltrated and Scotland unified into a proud nation. This was the centre from which Christianity, introduced by Columba into the little island of Iona, in conjunction with earlier but more localised missionaries, spread the Word not only throughout Scotland, but also to Lindisfarne on the Northumbrian coast, across the North Sea to the Low Countries and far up the Rhine, and through the Vikings to Scandinavia. Surely Argyll must be one of the most historical, and in the light of later events, one of the most romantic areas in Scotland. Early records of the Celtic race come next in antiquity in Europe to those of the Greeks and Romans.

Mid Argyll is the heart of Dalriada, rich in antiquities — chambered cairns, cup and ring marked rocks, standing stones, and the original fortress-capital Dunadd — and the later records of Christianity in chapels, sculptured crosses and tombstones, together with the lands and castles of the powerful clans that evolved after the twelfth century. Until the disruption of the Clan System in the seventeenth century and its dissolution after the Battle of Culloden in 1746, the system was described as the 'finest example of benevolent feudalism in Europe'. Certainly the power of certain independent western clans, notably the MacDonalds, in the consortium known as the Lords of the Isles, was an ever-present embarrassment to the Scottish Parliament, hence the building of military roads and forts which allowed Parliamentary troops the better to police these distant areas. Do not forget, however, that there was a logical reason for this unrest, and by the greater clans keeping lesser clans under control a measure of social stability was effected which otherwise might have been a rabble of lawlessness.

The first Celts, (pronounced 'Celts', not 'Kelts' which are spent or diseased salmon!) were early settlers from Ireland, a pastoral people who settled along the coasts and built these coastal forts as a defence against waves of later and more militant incomers. They became known as 'Scots' after Scota, who was mother of the great Irish leader Milesius just before the Roman invasion of England. Under Fergus, the survivor of three brothers who shared the lands of Lorne, Cowal and Kintyre, Dalriada became a separate kingdom which was recognised by the Picts — the original inhabitants — in return for a joint alliance against the Britons who were thrusting north from Strathclyde. In fact, if you are passing through Glen Falloch, at the north end of Loch Lomond, above and on the west side of the road not far from the Falls of Falloch you can see a great boulder called Clach nam Bretann, where the lands of the Scots, Picts and Britons were supposed to meet, not far from the later county boundaries of Argyll, Stirling and Perth. By the year 843 King Kenneth MacAlpine of Dalriada, through his marriage with the direct successor on the female side to the Pictish line, became first king of the unified Scots and Picts. The united territories became known as Scotland.

However, this book is designed to describe Argyll as it is today. It no longer stretches from the Mull of Kintyre to Wester Ross, although it is convenient to keep to that old definition, with apologies to Inverness-shire and Perthshire. Modern Argyll is now a part of the Strathclyde Region. Within its ancient bounds lie Ben Nevis (4406ft), highest mountain in Britain; Loch Morar (1017ft), deepest loch in Britain, and second deepest in Europe, exceeded by one lake in Scandinavia; Britain's longest loch, Loch Awe (25½ miles), and its loch with the greatest area of fresh water — Loch Lomond. You can also stretch a point and include lovely Loch Maree, in Wester Ross, the loch with the greatest area of islands. Argyll includes many islands of the Inner Hebrides, Islay, Jura, Colonsay, Gigha, Coll, Tiree, and the islands along the Firth of Lorne; but greatest of all it includes the Isle of Mull, with its own off-shore islands of Ulva, Gometra, Staffa, Iona, and the bird and seal sanctuaries of the Treshnish Islands. Its western coasts are dotted with the ruins of dozens of Iron Age forts.

Argyll is the land so vividly described by Boswell and Dr Johnson in the eighteenth century and by later writers like Robert Louis Stevenson and Neil Munro in their stirring tales of the past, in which we follow their heroes through the Ross of Mull, Appin, Glencoe, Lochaber, the Moor of Rannoch and the lands of Lorne. There is the peninsula of Ardnamurchan — 'Headland of the Great Waves' — most westerly point of Great Britain, with its red deer, golden eagles and wild cats, with white sandy bays biting into its grim dark rocky coasts. There are inlets and sea lochs where yachtsmen can relax at safe anchorages, for these coasts can be stormy and highly dangerous when the Atlantic gales blow up. There is Glencoe, with its towering mountains and the sad story of a deed of shameful treachery, but nowadays a centre for mountaineering, like Fort William. It was a natural decision during the war to adopt the rugged district north of Fort William as a training area for commando troops, to whose memory that fine memorial stands just beyond Spean Bridge.

Argyll today attracts increasing numbers of visitors to enjoy its infinite variety of interests, from archaeology to geology to sport and the study of wildlife. There is excellent angling for salmon, seatrout, brown and rainbow trout, and of course superlative sea angling. There is also mountaineering or hill walking, ski-ing in winter, with the modern ski-lift in Glencoe giving access to the high slopes, yachting, golf, pony-trekking, or simply quietly relaxing in an atmosphere far removed from the frenetic rush of the sophisticated south. The winding roads pass through scenes of unsurpassable beauty, where every turn of the road provides an opportunity for a photograph for the camera enthusiast.

Road distances seem long, for Argyll has many jutting peninsulas and deeply-penetrating sea lochs involving considerable detours; and of course in Oban we have the gateway to the western seas and islands. It is a busy place, whose hotels and accommodation cater for a large influx of visitors. Its rival is Fort William, another centre but for different interests, from which roads radiate into the fastnesses of the Western Highlands — the romantic Road to the Isles and the land of Prince Charlie — or eastwards into the central Highlands, with the Caledonian Canal stretching from the head of Loch Linnhe by the Great Glen and its lochs to Inverness and the Moray Firth.

Mull is only 40 minutes from Oban by the frequent 50-car ferry. It is an island where time stands still, where the roads go up and the mists come down, whose roads have only one or two white guiding lines, no yellow lines, no traffic wardens; perhaps only a green line along the centre of some of the side roads — the worn grass and rushes. Although well-surfaced, the roads, apart from a section of new motor road, are narrow, with passing places, blind corners and sharp gradients. The main-road motorist must show extra care, courtesy and consideration. On unfenced roads here, and throughout the Highlands, do beware of livestock, for sheep and cattle can act unpredictably and suddenly. Crofters and sheep farmers are by no means affluent men, and young lambs killed on the roads by passing motorists in summer can add up to a considerable loss when the autumn sales come along, for by then these helpless lambs would have grown up and fetched a price of £20 each and upwards at today's prices. Furthermore, a dead lamb jammed in the steering of a car has sent many a vehicle off the road.

The inhabitants of the Highlands and Islands are a quiet, soft-spoken, friendly and hospitable race once the visitor gets to know them. However, he is well advised to prepare to adjust to their tempo of life. This is brought out in the story of a visitor from Spain who once enquired of an old local man, 'Tell me, have you any word in the Gaelic language equivalent to our Spanish word *Mañana*?'

The old man considered the question for a long, long time; then removing his pipe and refilling it, which gave him time to think, he replied, 'Indeed, there iss no word in the Gaelic language with such urgency!'

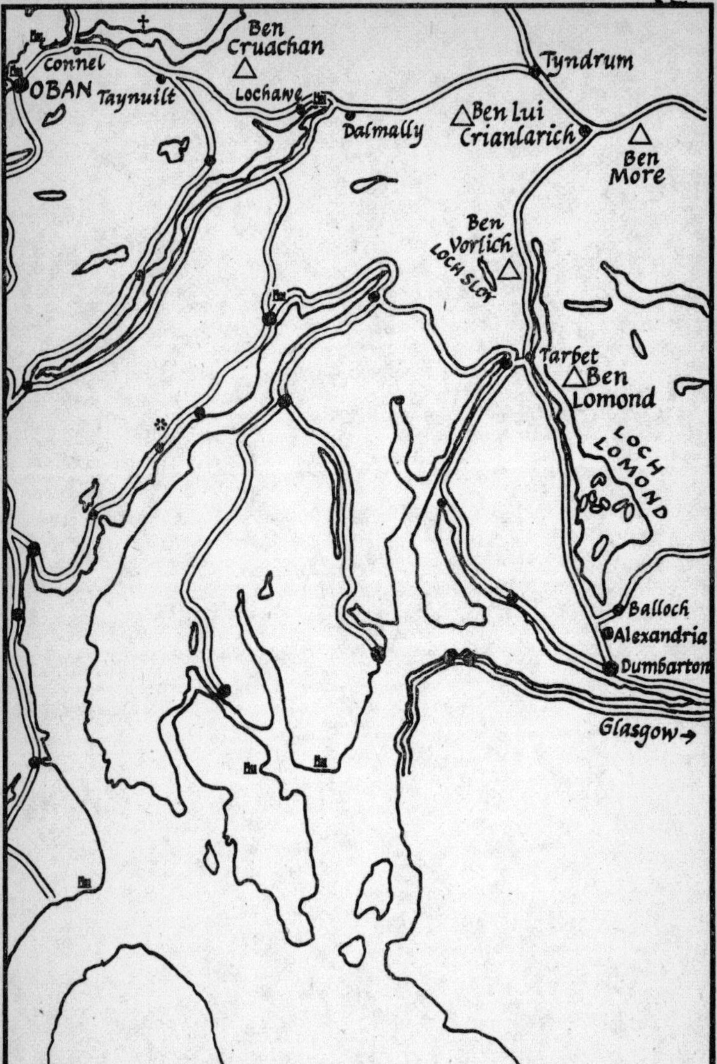
Ben Cruachan
Connel
OBAN
Taynuilt
Lochawe
Dalmally
Tyndrum
Ben Lui
Crianlarich
Ben More
Ben Vorlich
LOCH SLOY
Tarbet
Ben Lomond
LOCH LOMOND
Balloch
Alexandria
Dumbarton
Glasgow →

Glasgow to Oban via Loch Lomond (93 miles)

THE CONVENTIONAL ROAD FROM Glasgow and the south to Oban and the West Highlands is by Balloch, Loch Lomond, Tarbet, Crianlarich, Tyndrum and Dalmally. Until the Erskine Bridge over the Clyde was opened, traffic from Ayrshire and Greenock crossed the river by the old Erskine Ferry, described by a cynical Norwegian as an 'antiquated raft', which hauled itself to and fro along chains that normally lay on the bed of the river.

The road from Balloch runs along the whole western shore of Loch Lomond. This is a busy road now — certainly during the day and in the holiday season — thronged with tourist traffic on top of the usual commercial vehicles, for this is also Glasgow's commercial outlet to the north-west. Road improvements have quite failed to keep up with the traffic flow, and the many visitors travelling by car to see the famed scenery and 'Bonnie Bonnie Banks' of Loch Lomond see little for twenty tortuous miles but the number plate of the car in front and tantalising glimpses through a screen of scrub bushes of the beauties of the loch, its islands, its own cruise ship *Maid of the Loch* that sails daily from Balloch pier — an excellent way of exploring the loch although it is under threat of being discontinued at the time of writing — and the peak of Ben Lomond (3192ft) dominating the opposite shores. With many narrow bridges and a lack of parking spaces this part of the road is disappointing and dangerous. Later we shall tell you of an attractive alternative. However, nothing can detract from the natural beauties of hill and loch and the leisurely traveller can still find a corner to draw in and look around.

At Luss, a short distance north of Balloch, we pass through the clan lands of the Colquhouns. In 1603 Glen Fruin was the scene of a fierce fight, one of the last inter-clan fights in the Highlands, between that clan and the MacGregors. The losses suffered by the Colquhouns were so dreadful that sixty widows, carrying as evidence the blood-stained shirts of their slain husbands, appeared before King James VI at Stirling, and demanded vengeance. The Court was shocked; the outcome was a decree that all members of the Clan MacGregor were to be proscribed, outlawed, killed on sight and their lands forfeited. This persecution of a once great clan lasted until the decree was repealed in 1795.

The road continues past Tarbet (the name, which occurs frequently, means an isthumus or neck of land) about halfway up the west side, where Magnus, Viking King of Man, had his galley dragged on rollers overland from Loch Long, then by sailing down Loch Lomond and back to the Clyde by the River Leven, he claimed all this land he had thus circumnavigated.

At Inveruglas, where the modern power station stands, Glen Sloy opens westwards towards Loch Sloy, whose waters are piped down to the power station. This is MacFarlane country, and their warcry was 'Loch Sloy'. Secure in the fastnesses of this nest of 3000-foot mountains, the clan became notorious for stealing cattle from neighbouring clans. In fact, the full moon was known as 'MacFarlane's Lantern', for its light presented the raiders with ideal conditions for their operations. After the '45 Jacobite uprising, when the carrying of weapons was prohibited in the Highlands, the order was waived in the case of drovers, who were allowed to arm themselves against likely attacks from cattle thieves.

Loch Lomond pinches out at Ardlui and the road climbs up Glen Falloch to the open glens above, passing the Falls of Falloch in about three miles. Opposite the Falls, on the steep slope on the west side of the road, not far from Inverarnan and north-west of the railway line, stands a great boulder called Clach nam Bretann to which we referred earlier. It is said to have marked where the kingdom of the Scots, Picts and Britons met. In upper Glen Falloch you will see a remnant of the old Caledonian Forest of Scots pine that once covered much of the land. In another three miles we come to the hamlet of Crianlarich, which is overlooked to the east by the twin peaks of Ben More (3843ft) and Stobinian (3821ft). As mountains feature so prominently in any description of Scotland, it might be appropriate to define a 'Munro'. This word, which you will often come across, denotes a mountain of 3000 feet or more in height, or an individual peak in a group, divided from its nearest neighbour by a drop of at least 500 feet.

The term derives from the name of the man who first listed them. There are about 276 'Munroes' in Scotland.

We have not mentioned the railway so far. This runs from Glasgow along the Clyde by Dumbarton and Helensburgh, crosses the isthmus to Loch Lomond and thereafter closely follows the line of the road to Crianlarich. Here it forks, one branch continuing to Oban, the other crossing the valley, striking north from Tyndrum (The House by the Pass) and weaving its way across the Moor of Rannoch to Fort William and Mallaig. It will be a sad day if the threat of closing these lines is implemented, for apart from their use as local life-lines, the Mallaig section in particular should be developed and publicised as one of the most scenic routes in Europe.

From Crianlarich the road turns west through Strathfillan, called after the Celtic saint of that name, formerly the land of the Clans Dewar and Macnab which were both of ecclesiastic origin. About a mile from Tyndrum, to the left of the road, lies the battlefield of Dalrigh (King's Field) where at the beginning of the 14th century King Robert the Bruce was confronted by a body of MacDougalls and Macnabs, clans that opposed him because of his sacrilege in murdering the Red Comyn, another claimant to the throne, in a church at Dumfries. Bruce was hard pressed but escaped by killing his chief attacker, in whose dying clutch, however, he was obliged to leave his cloak in which was fixed the famous Brooch of Lorne as it came to be called, which is still in the hands of the MacDougalls at Dunollie, Oban.

We continue past the road junction at Tyndrum along Glen Lochy to Dalmally and

Loch Awe, lands of the Campbells of Breadalbane and Glen Orchy. Around Dalmally the land is more open and fertile. Above Dalmally railway station stands the ruined village of Barachaistelain (Castle Place on the Ridge) where a sept of the Macnabs lived from the early fifteenth century. They were hereditary smiths and armourers, an important and highly respected occupation in the Middle Ages, to the Campbells of Breadalbane. In 1440 they made and installed all the ironwork during the rebuilding of Kilchuirn Castle, that picturesque ruin which stands on a marshy promontory, once an island, at the eastern side of the head of Loch Awe. A well-known prediction about the family was long current, to the effect that when the last son to succeed his father as hereditary smith should die, an old elm whose mighty branches overshadowed the smithy would fall. This prediction was fulfilled towards the end of the eighteenth century. On the night when the old man lay dying a great storm swept the glen. In the morning he was dead and the old elm lay in front of the smithy. As time went on all the sons left the village and the smithy fell into disuse.

About two miles south-west of Dalmally, above the old road to Inveraray, stands a prominent four-square monument surmounted by a low open tower, erected in memory of the bard Duncan Ban MacIntyre (1724-1812), the humble shepherd-gamekeeper and Gaelic poet, sometimes called the Bard of the North. Illiterate, but with a remarkable memory and imagination, he composed poetry, first published in 1768, which included some of the finest compositions of any Scottish poet.

Beyond Dalmally lies long narrow Loch Awe,

whose name is derived from Gaelic *Abhainn*, a river. In past geological ages the loch had its outlet at the south end, near Ford; but blocked off by glaciers, and with the water standing at a higher level, it cut a new outlet to the north-west through what is now the Pass of Brander, where the River Awe of the big salmon rushes north into Loch Etive.

We are now well into the land of Argyll and its castles. The first castle of note is Kilchuirn, built about the fourteenth century by Sir Colin Campbell, founder of the Breadalbane family, although some authorities suggest it was originally a MacGregor stronghold. The once great power of this influential Campbell family is satirised in a poem about one particular Marquis which begins:

From Kenmore to Ben More
The Land is a' the Markis's;
Each heathery knowe, ilk' mossy howe
And every bonny park is his.

The crofter's rent, the tinkler's tent,
The ghillie's hard day's wark is his;
From Kenmore to Ben More
The folk is a' the Markis's . . .

The road passes along the north shore of Loch Awe, squeezed in between the water and the railway by the precipitous slopes of Ben Cruachan, whose group of seven peaks, rising to a height of 3689 feet, stands boldly isolated above. There are two main tops, the Dalmally Peak (Cruachan Beann 3689ft) which is the principal peak and the Taynuilt Peak (Stob Dearg 3611ft). They are connected by a ridge three-quarters of a mile in length. The ascent, which can be particularly rewarding, can be made either from the Oban side at Bridge of Awe, or to the east peak reached from the road to the dam above the Falls of Cruachan.

The little church of St Conan's is well worth a visit. It stands just above the shore of the loch in the middle of the village that straggles along the narrow, tree-lined road. Although completed as recently as 1930 by a local family, it is of unique construction and contains many objects of interest and some attractive ornamental ironwork. There is a miniature 'Thistle Chapel' reminiscent of St Giles, Edinburgh, where there are two sets of stalls in dark wood facing each other, each stall bearing the name of one of the local clan chiefs.

A Hydro-Electric generating station now stands where the loch begins to narrow in the Pass of Brander. It is powered by water conveyed from the dam built 1315 feet up in a corrie of Ben Cruachan, access to which is provided by a private road, available for use by the public on application. The Falls of Cruachan lie just below the dam. This was the first project of its kind in Scotland, where a pumped-storage design uses the surplus power at off-peak periods to reverse the flow of water for re-storage in the dam. The mountain has been tunnelled and a great underground cavern excavated to house generators.

This is a fine new road passing through the Pass of Brander above the edge of the water which here drops by underwater cliffs to a depth of up to 250 feet just a few yards off the shore. The dark-shadowed rocks and precipitous screes of the opposite side give the place an air of gloom, even in the summer months.

Near the low dam at the outflow there was another desperate battle in 1308 between the MacDougalls of Lorne and King Robert the Bruce when Bruce avenged his defeat at Dalrigh. The battleground is marked by a few low cairns.

Before we leave Loch Awe, mention should be made of the old tale about the Great Beast of the loch, a twelve-legged something between an eel and a horse. When the loch was covered with ice strange cracks and sounds sometimes were heard echoing across the loch. These made local folks look at each other with apprehension, saying to each other that the Great Beast was trying to break out.

About four miles from the end of the loch we come to Taynuilt (The House by the River) and for the first time see and scent the salt water of the western seas. The River Awe flows into Loch Etive about a mile from the village. This is one of Scotland's great salmon rivers, where fish of up to 56 lbs have been caught by rod and line. A side road takes you to the old furnace works where iron was smelted, using local wood to fire the furnace. It took five tons of timber or a ton of coal to produce a ton of pig iron, using iron ore from Lancashire. This work started here on the south shore of Loch Etive as early as 1753, in an effort to bring some form of industry to the Highlands. It operated until 1873 and by this time much of the timber in the district had been cut down to make charcoal. Scottish woodlands were supposed to have been protected but this was completely ignored by ironworkers in England, who set up about 100 such iron works in Scotland after the '45 uprising, when Scotland was given over to exploitation. Thus many of the old woodlands disappeared, hastened, too, by the demand for charcoal to make explosives.

Loch Etive is a long narrow sea loch stretching for 18 miles north-east towards Glen Etive and Glen Coe, with no roads, only a few tracks, along its upper shores. Opposite Taynuilt, on the north side of Loch Etive, can be seen the scar of the great Bonawe Quarry, from which much of the graded road metal and surfacing materials for Argyll roads is shipped out by small coasters.

This loch is prominent in old Celtic literature. Away at the head of the loch, between that point and the south end of the mountain Buchaille Etive Mor (Great Herdsman of Etive) lies the sunny slope where stood the dwelling place of the legendary Deirdre of the Sorrows, who had fled from Ireland with her lover, Naoise, to avoid a forced marriage to another. Here they settled happily, roaming the hills, hunting the deer and catching the salmon in the pools, until tragedy struck. Being invited to return to Ireland under safe conduct, Naoise was treacherously murdered, whereupon Deirdre took her own life. This is surely one of the saddest of old Celtic legends.

Skirting the shore of Loch Etive we come to the railway bridge spanning the narrows at Connel Ferry. This originally carried the branch line to Ballachulish, long since closed, and has been converted to carry the main road from Connel Ferry to Appin and Fort William. When the railway operated, road traffic was allowed to use the bridge on payment of a toll, which was most unpopular locally. Far to the west we can see for the first time the outline of the blue mountains of Mull. Below the bridge itself lie what are called the Falls of Lora, where the tides of Loch Etive at certain stages of the flow pour over a sunken ledge in a sea-cataract. The bridge was built in 1903 to replace the dangerous ferry crossing and now, as a road bridge, it is of great social and economic value to the whole district, especially for the passage of livestock.

Across the bridge, on the north side of the loch lies Ardchattan Priory, founded in 1230 by Duncan MacCoul, progenitor of the MacDougalls. Just across the bridge, too, on the flat Moss of Achnacree, there is the airstrip that serves the district around Oban.

Two miles nearer Oban lies another Campbell stronghold, the Castle of Dunstaffnage, on the promontory across the bay of that name. It belonged originally to the MacDougalls, but became part of the Campbell lands when Colin Campbell, First Earl of Argyll, married Isabella Stewart, daughter of the last Lord of Lorne. It was built as a fort by an early descendant of Somerled, Lord of the Isles. The cruelty and perfidy common in the Middle Ages is exemplified by the murder of old Coll (*Ciotach*) MacDonald of Islay. He was the governor of the castle of Dunnyveg when it was threatened with capture by Campbell, the Captain of Dunstaffnage, who was in fact an old friend of the MacDonald. Friendship went by the board. Under an offer of parole, Coll came out in good faith but was seized, taken captive to Dunstaffnage, and hanged from the mast of his own galley which they laid across a cleft in the rocks near the castle.

The Stone of Destiny — Jacob's Pillow — the Lia Fail, said to have been brought over from Ireland to Dunadd by Fergus Mor, first King of Dalriada, was transferred to Dunstaffnage and remained there until Kenneth MacAlpine removed it to Scone, where it was built into a wooden chair for his coronation in 844. Together with other Scottish loot it was removed to England by Edward I in 1296 and although its return was embodied in the Treaty of Union of 1707, this was never implemented. Today it still lies below the Coronation Chair in Westminster Abbey. However, after its unofficial removal and return some years ago there are doubts as to whether or not the present stone is in fact the original.

Flora MacDonald, who so successfully helped Prince Charlie to escape from the Outer Isles, was imprisoned at Dunstaffnage for a time in 1746.

In Dunstaffnage Bay there is a Marine Biological Station where a wide selection of sea life can be seen in its natural habitat.

About four miles later Oban is reached. A sign *Ceud Mile Failte* (100,000 Welcomes) greets the traveller at a blind corner — and round it and below lie the town and magnificent Bay of Oban with the sheltering island of Kerrera behind, and beyond it the open Firth of Lorne and the island of Mull. Oban has been variously described as the 'Charing Cross of the Highlands', the 'Gateway to the Hebrides', and more disputably the 'Capital of the Highlands'. Inverness would dispute that with justification! It has been a rail terminus since 1883, and is a centre for both the fishing fleet and for communications with the Hebridean islands. Major livestock sales are held here in the market. Oban, however, is best known as a tourist centre, one of the most popular in Scotland, with hotels, shops and guest houses catering for the annual influx of visitors.

Although in these days of economic pressures MacBrayne's fleet of cargo and passenger vessels, once centred in Oban, is a shadow of what it used to be, there are still regular sailings to Mull, Coll, Tiree, Barra, and lesser islands. Mull is served by a modern roll-on roll-off car ferry with five daily return journeys in the season, two in winter.

Although rather shallow in places, Oban Bay is a sheltered stretch of water much frequented by yachtsmen and of course the fishing fleets. It is well protected by the island of Kerrera, which is passed by the main channel to the north and by the Sound of Kerrera to the south. There was some talk of bridging the Sound of Kerrera — a far cry from the days when droves of black cattle, the former wealth of the islands, used to be ferried across from Mull to Kerrera, then swum across the narrow Sound to the mainland and their long journey to the fairs and markets of the south.

Oban, with its hospital and homes, is a medical centre for the whole area. It is also a centre for Higher Education at the High School. One unfortunate outcome of this modern centralisation of education is that youngsters at an early and impressionable age have to leave their homes in remoter districts where formerly there was the village school, to go to school elsewhere, returning home most weekends. This unsettling factor diverts them from any wish to settle near their homes, even if job opportunities are available.

Oban has its distillery, a tweed mill and a glassware business. The town is dominated by a strange 'Folly', McCaig's Tower, building of which was started in 1897 by John S McCaig, a banker and philanthropist, to provide local employment. It was designed as a museum, and the many windows were to have held statues of members of his family. Unfortunately McCaig died before more than the outer shell had been built, and the project had to be abandoned.

The town is not of great antiquity, having been established as a fishing village in the eighteenth century, although judging from local archaeological finds, there must have been a small settlement there from prehistoric times. At the north end of the Bay, on a rock, stands the ivy-covered ruin of Dunollie Castle, built in the twelfth or thirteenth century as a defensive position by the MacDougalls, Lords of Lorne. They were descended from Loarn, brother of that Fergus who founded Dalriada. Below the castle, beside the road that skirts the shore on the way to Ganavan sands, stands a tall isolated pillar of rock much undercut by the sea when it stood at a higher level. This is the Dog Stone, or *Clach a'Choin* as it is called in Gaelic, and tradition has it that Bran, the hunting hound of the giant Fingal, used to be chained here, the chain wearing deeply into the base of the rock. Alternatively, it is said that when the Lord of the Isles used to visit Dunollie, his hunting dogs were secured near the stone. The mansion house of Dunollie lies not far from the old castle, and in it the Brooch of Lorne, already mentioned, and other interesting relics are preserved by the MacDougalls. The brooch was in the hands of Campbell families from 1647 but was generously returned in 1826.

Along the coasts of Argyll, the Sound of Mull, and parts of western Mull, there are excellent examples of raised beaches, such as the platform on which the Dog Stone stands. These were formed when the sea stood at a higher level for long enough to wear down the rocks between periods when the land was slowly rising after being relieved of its deep and heavy ice cap.

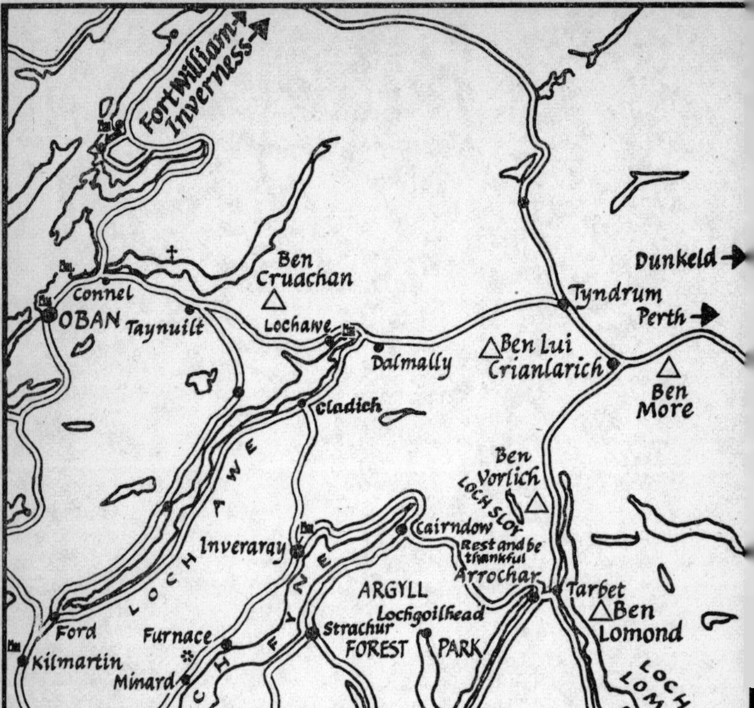

Fort William
Inverness
Ben Cruachan
Connel
OBAN
Taynuilt
Lochawe
Dalmally
Ben Lui
Crianlarich
Tyndrum
Dunkeld
Perth
Ben More
Cladich
Ben Vorlich
LOCH SLOY
LOCH AWE
Inveraray
Cairndow
Rest and be thankful
Arrochar
Tarbet
Ben Lomond
ARGYLL
Lochgoilhead
Ford
Furnace
Strachur
FOREST PARK
Kilmartin
Minard
LOCH FYNE
LOCH LOMOND
Gairlochhead
Lochgair
Lochgilphead
LOCH LONG
GAIR LOCH
Helensburgh
Stirling
Balloch
Alexandria
L. GILP
LOCH STRIVEN
Dunoon
Greenock
Dumbarton
Gourock
Colintraive
FIRTH OF CLYDE
Ayr
Glasgow
Edinburgh
BUTE

Into Argyll from other parts of Scotland: Alternative road by Inveraray

From Dunkeld and the Central Highlands

DUNKELD IS AN IMPORTANT CENTRE ON the main road to the north of Scotland from Perth to Inverness. This old town links up with the west by Aberfeldy and Loch Tay. At Aberfeldy the River Tay is crossed by the famous bridge, built in 1733 by William Adam, General Wade's architect. Note, when passing, the monument erected here in 1887 to the Black Watch regiment, the 42nd, which was begun in 1667 by a few Highland chiefs as a local militia to preserve the peace. Their uniform was designed in a dark colour (hence the 'Black') to avoid confusion with the hated red uniforms of the English troops, or Redcoats, as they were universally called.

From Aberfeldy the road follows the north side of Loch Tay. If time allows, a short detour can be made to the mouth of Glen Lyon, Scotland's longest glen, by branching west from the north-east end of the loch. Here stands the trim village of Fortingal, where there is a yew tree reputed to be over 2000 years old. This was a settlement far back into pre-history, with cup-marked rocks, standing stones and a burial tumulus. Some people still believe that Pontius Pilate was born here and that his mother was a local woman; certainly his father was an ambassador in the Highland area during Roman times, and what are thought to be the remains of a Roman camp are situated here. Here, too, stands the house of the family of Campbell of Glenlyon who was involved in the massacre of Glencoe.

At the west end of Loch Tay the road passes through Killin, crossing the River Dochart flowing into Loch Tay, by the bridge that divides the old village from the new. In former times this was the centre — the *Duthus* or hearth-stone, as it used to be called — of the Clan Macnab. Their burial island, Inch Buie, carries a section of the bridge that also spans the well-known Falls of Dochart. When evil times fell on the clan this island was for a time the only portion of land they possessed. Following the destruction by Cromwell of their keep at Eilean Ran, at the mouth of the River Lochy nearby, a new residence was built in 1580 at Kinnell House, half a mile down the river on the right-hand bank. In front of Kinnell stands the miniature cannon which were used to fire a salute to welcome Queen Victoria when she visited Loch Tay. In the conservatory attached to the house grows what used to be the longest vine in Europe (190 feet) and although now much reduced in length it still bears good crops of grapes.

Killin is in the land of St Fillan and certain stones with alleged healing qualities which are said to have belonged to the Saint are still preserved in the village. About four miles up Glen Dochart the road joins the Oban road at

Lix Toll, so called because from there it was LIX or 59 miles from Glasgow.

From Perth

From Perth the traveller heads for Crieff and along Scotland's 'Rift Valley' to Comrie and St Fillans, where minor earth tremors occur from time to time. Loch Earn stretches westwards from St Fillans, and the road follows the north side to Lochearnhead, on the Oban road.

There is one tale of savagery in the sixteenth century that comes from Loch Earn. Just off St Fillans you will see Neish Island out in the loch. This was the island stronghold of the Clan Neish, one of the lesser clans. One December they waylaid a party of Macnabs carrying provisions to Killin and after beating up the servants appropriated the loads. Much wroth, and on the challenge of their father, six Macnab sons carried a boat in mid-winter all the way across the hills from Loch Tay to Loch Earn, for the Neishes had secured every boat on Loch Earn and tied them up at their island. Launching their boat, the Macnabs rowed along the loch, landed on Neish island and stormed the dwelling where in fancied security, the Neishes were carousing on the stolen spirits and provender. Every one was put to the sword except for a child that was missed under an overturned crib — and the Macnab sons returned to Killin bearing in a sack the head of the Neish chief which they threw at their father the chief's feet as evidence of their revengeful action. Even those mighty men were so hard stressed that on the return journey they were obliged to leave the boat high up in the hills, where it lay until its timbers rotted away. After this bloodthirsty incident the Macnabs adopted a savage's head in their crest.

Past Lochearnhead, on the way to Oban, the road climbs up bare, rocky Glen Ogle, described by Queen Victoria as the 'Khyber Pass of the Highlands', and on to Crianlarich.

Roads from Edinburgh, Fife and the longer road from Glasgow by Stirling

All these roads converge at Stirling and from there the road to Oban and Fort William continues through Dunblane and Doune. It touches the eastern section of the Trossachs at Callander, another popular tourist centre, often also described as the 'Gateway to the Highlands'. It is certainly a picturesque approach to the woods, lochs and mountains of The Trosssachs, so well described in Scott's *Lady of the Lake* and other writings.

The Falls of Leny, another beauty spot, lie two miles beyond Callander, then the road goes along the eastern shore of Loch Lubnaig, another of these deep narrow Highland lochs, through 'Bonnie Strathyre' of the song, with its extensive forestry plantations, past Balquhidder, with its memories of the great Rob Roy, then on to Lochearnhead and the roads already described.

Dunkeld to Oban, 97 miles; Glasgow to Oban by Stirling, 115 miles; Glasgow to Oban by Crianlarich, 105 miles; Perth to Oban, 95 miles.

Alternative road to Oban by Greenock from Edinburgh and Glasgow

Earlier in the book we condemned a section of the conventional road from Glasgow to Oban along Loch Lomond. Let us now describe the route we recommend.

A fast motorway (M8) now extends from Edinburgh and the South through the heart of Glasgow past the airport, almost to the port of Greenock. At Gourock, a mile or two beyond, there is, at the time of writing, a choice of two excellent ferries to Dunoon, on the Cowal shore of Argyll. It is a crossing of about 20 minutes with the bonus of a look at the sea traffic on this busy waterway. The distance from Dunoon to Oban is 80 miles and the road is excellent (except for four miles of reconstruction beyond Inveraray) with little traffic. It is a road to enjoy, on which to linger, or make up time at the whim of the driver, through scenery fully comparable with that of the Loch Lomond road, and it is little longer in mileage.

Dunoon, although in Argyll, is far from the heart of that county. The road skirts the Holy Loch with a close-up view of the depot ships of the Nuclear Submarine Base there, and in a mile or two comes to the Younger Arboretum and Gardens which are well worth a visit. Just beyond lies Loch Eck, long and narrow, like Loch Lubnaig, but with more contrasting loveliness, with higher hills, dark woods and deep still waters. Pushing on, we come to the fresh salty air of Loch Fyne — 16 miles from Dunoon — at Strachur, where the old Creggans Inn beside the little ruined pier, is a good place to stop for morning coffee or afternoon tea. The inn is run by Sir Fitzroy Maclean, of war-time fame in Yugoslavia, and Lady Maclean.

From there it is twenty-five delightful miles to Inveraray, passing Cairndow, where the road from Glasgow by Tarbet and Arrocher joins in (see notes towards the end of this chapter). We cross the new structures that by-pass the picturesque old high-arched bridges at the mouths of Glen Fyne and Glen Shira. Between the bridges, before we round Strone Point, stands the castle of Dundarave (Dun da Ramh, the Fort of the Two Oars), a MacNaughton stronghold until taken over by the Clan Campbell. It is the Doom Castle of Neil Munro's writings and has featured in television serials in recent years.

Neil Munro (1864-1930), that versatile writer who was born in Inveraray, vividly described the Loch Fyne country and Mid Argyll in such books as *John Splendid*, *The New Road*, *The Lost Pibroch*, and of course *The Vital Spark*, in which he recounts the stories of that venerable steam lighter, or 'puffer' as they were known along the west coast, and her wily skipper Para Handy. We can almost visualise the puffer pushing Loch Fyne in front of her, flat out at seven knots with the steam valve tied down with rope!

The town of Inveraray is approached by the old arched bridge built by the 5th Duke of Argyll between 1770 and 1780 across the River Aray below the castle, residence of the Duke of Argyll and heart of the Clan Campbell.

The present town of Inveraray was built in 1745. The then Duke of Argyll wished to build a new castle, the third such building on the site — the first was a fourteenth-century tower built by Cailean Mor when the Campbell lands were centred on Loch Awe — but as he considered the proximity of the town would spoil the amenity of the new castle he had the nearest houses pulled down and re-erected where they now stand. You will see the old courthouse where in 1752 James of the Glen was convicted of the murder of Colin

Campbell of Glenure, a crime of which he was innocent, before a Campbell judge and a Campbell jury. The Campbells had no love for the Stewarts, and James was one of them. He was sentenced to death by hanging from a gibbet erected near the site of the murder at Ballachulish. The incident has been known ever since as the Appin Murder. Robert Louis Stevenson used the murder as part of the plot in his *Kidnapped* and *Catriona*.

Robert Burns visited the town: in fact, he vented his disapproval of being cold-shouldered by the hotel management in favour of distinguished Campbell guests by writing his famous lines on a window pane in the Argyll Hotel:

There's naething here but Hielan' pride,
An' Hielan' scab, an' hunger;
If Providence has sent me here,
'Twere surely in his anger.

The Campbells were regarded with a certain contempt by other clans, sometimes with justification, for their policy was to run with the hare and hunt with the hounds. They always backed the Government of the day, although not without the risk of a sudden reversal of national policy such as that which cost one great Marquis of Argyll his head. But however crafty were their machinations, with no lack of the cruelties and treacheries common to the age, they were brave fighting men and like the Lords of the Isles they kept in order the lesser clans that came under their sphere of influence. It must be remembered that most of the other clans made the mistake of holding their lands by the sword instead of adopting the sensible Campbell method of having ownership legally recorded. Hence the contemptuous — or jealous? — reference by their over-proud critics to the 'Campbells and their Sheepskins'!, meaning the sheepskins or parchments on which deeds were officially recorded.

Inveraray Castle is a fine building in an attractive setting beside the River Aray. Although much damaged by a fire in modern times, it contains priceless relics, weapons and pictures from the past. It is open to the public and attracts crowds of interested visitors. Above it stands the steep hillock of Dun Cuaich with its tower from which in the old days watchers kept a look-out, such as in the days of Montrose in the seventeenth century, when the avenging MacDonalds came storming down Glen Aray with fire and sword.

The road from Glasgow to Campbeltown passes along the main street and continues by the shore towards Lochgilphead. The Oban road leaves the town through a narrow archway, and climbs up Glen Aray through the woods above the castle, past the fishponds, where a section of the old road is under reconstruction at present. Near the watershed, standing high above the road, there is the tall monument erected in memory of Neil Munro, looking back down the glen to the land he loved and wrote about.

The outlook from the highest point of the road must be one of the most magnificent in Scotland. Below, the line of the road winds down towards Loch Awe and its islands, here at its widest point. The black gash of the Pass of Brander is over to the west, Glen Strae and the former lands of the MacGregors lie to the right, and between them can be seen Ben Cruachan and its seven peaks, with the raw line of the access road to the dam slanting halfway up.

We continue down the hill to Cladich near the side of the loch, where a road cuts to the left towards Ford, at the south end of the loch, and Lochgilphead. Then we go through the woods, with Loch Awe glinting to the left, and we come in sight of Kilchuirn Castle, where the River Orchy enters the loch. After Eilean Donnan Kilchuirn is perhaps one of the most photographed of Scotland's old castles in the western Highlands.

Just west of Dalmally we join the main Oban road from Crianlarich for the remaining 24 miles to Oban.

Glasgow to Inveraray via Arrocher and the Rest-and-be-Thankful

There is still another road linking Glasgow-Crianlarich with the Inveraray road. On reaching Tarbet, Loch Lomond, instead of continuing up the shores of the loch towards Ardlui, turn left at the hotel and drive for two miles across the neck of land to Arrocher, which stands at the head of Loch Long. From here the well-graded modern road, following the line of the old military road, climbs up Glen Croe to the 'Rest-and-be-Thankful'. The summit is so called because the severity of the climb up the old road with its gradients and hairpin bends made the wayfarer rest and give thanks when he reached the top. The old road is still used for motor car hill tests. At the summit you will see a stone engraved with details of the building of the road by soldiers in 1768. There used to be a rough stone seat, but that is gone. This is a convenient and popular centre for Glasgow and district climbing enthusiasts exploring the group of peaks towering above Arrocher and 'The Rest': Ben Ime, Ben Arthur (better known as 'The Cobbler' from its configuration), and neighbouring hills all around 3000 feet.

The road descends Glen Kinglas and joins the Dunoon-Inveraray road, just described, at Cairndow, beside Loch Fyne. Tarbet to Cairndow is 15 miles. This is in fact part of the long, long road (134 miles) from Glasgow to Campbeltown and the Mull of Kintyre.

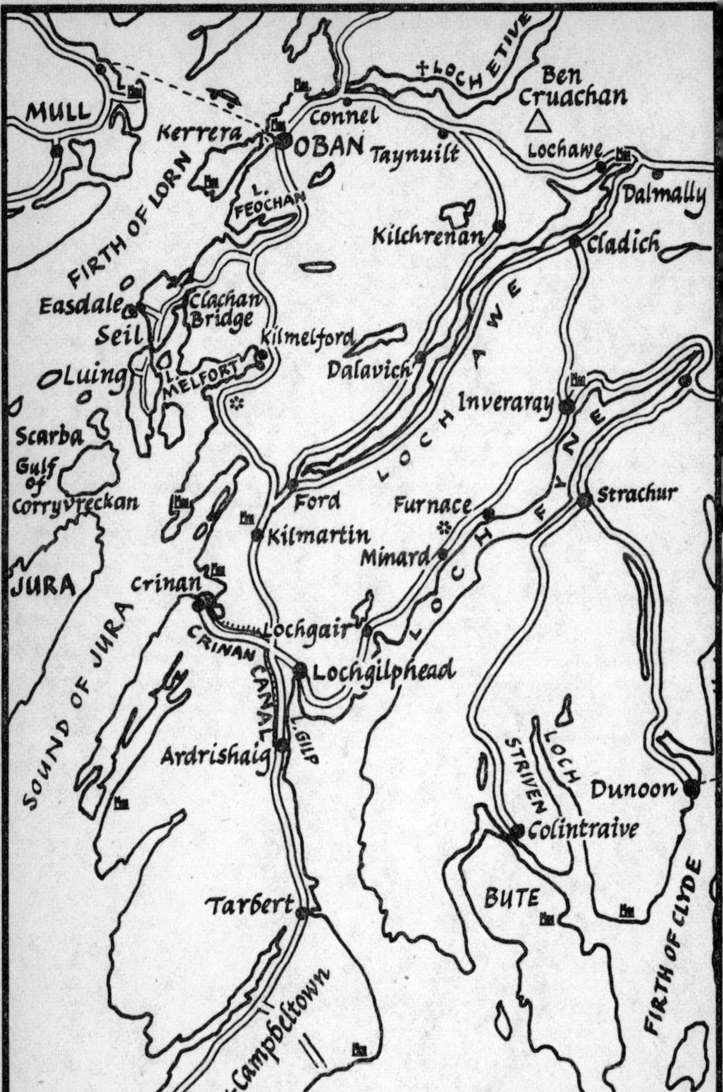
MULL
Kerrera
OBAN
Connel
LOCH ETIVE
Ben Cruachan
Taynuilt
Lochawe
Dalmally
L. FEOCHAN
FIRTH OF LORN
Kilchrenan
Cladich
Easdale
Clachan Bridge
Seil
Kilmelford
Luing
L. MELFORT
Dalavich
LOCH AWE
Inveraray
Scarba
Gulf of Corryvreckan
Ford
Furnace
Strachur
Kilmartin
Minard
LOCH FYNE
JURA
Crinan
Lochgair
CRINAN CANAL
SOUND OF JURA
Lochgilphead
L. GILP
Ardrishaig
LOCH STRIVEN
Dunoon
Colintraive
BUTE
Tarbert
FIRTH OF CLYDE
Campbeltown

Oban to Lochgilphead (37 miles)

LEAVING OBAN FROM BELOW THAT favourite vantage point, Pulpit Hill, a good road runs south into the heart of ancient Dalriada to Lochgilphead and from there to Campbeltown to the south and Inveraray to the east. It follows the coastline of the Firth of Lorne, with its sea lochs and offshore islands, opening out to the wide Atlantic. It skirts the lochs of Feochan, Melford and Craignish, with magnificent views westwards. Eight miles south, at Kilninver, we branch to the right to explore the slate islands of Seil, Luing and Easdale. The road crosses the Sound of Seil by the single high-arched bridge of Clachan, better known as the 'Bridge over the Atlantic', which was an important link with the mainland when the slate industry on Seil and Easdale was at its height. The bridge was built in 1792 to a design by Telford. With the recession in demand for high-quality roofing slates the industry languished, and some of the deep quarries, excavated to well below sea level, became flooded. There is still some work going on at the Balvicar quarry on Seil.

Luing is the home of a special breed of Highland cattle bred in recent years to produce a more rapidly maturing type of this hardy animal. At Cullipool, in the north-west of the island, a large dam was built as a storage pond for an immense reserve of lobsters which is drawn upon as required for home and foreign markets.

This island group extends south to the high rugged island of Scarba, which is separated from the larger island of Jura, with its extensive sporting facilities, by the sailors' nightmare — especially in the days of sail — the Gulf of Corrievrechan, the most dangerous stretch of water in the British Isles. At certain combinations of wind and tide the roar of this vast ocean whirlpool can be heard ten miles and more away.

Another name connected with the dreaded Gulf is 'Breacain's Cooking Pot'. It is said that a Norwegian prince, Breacain, was set a test by the Lord of the Isles before he would give his daughter to the prince in marriage. According to the conditions of the test, Breacain was to remain in his galley anchored in the Gulf for the space of three days. If he survived, the marriage would be approved. On the advice of wise men back home in Norway, he had three ropes made which he hoped would provide ample reserve for anchoring. The first rope was of wool, and it parted the first day, to be replaced by the second, which was of hemp. This broke on the second day, but the third, a rope made of the hair of maidens of undoubted chastity, successfully took its place. Unfortunately, on the third and final day this rope also parted; unknown to the weavers of the rope, certain tresses had been included from the head of a maiden who at one time had departed from grace. This of course destroyed the magic strength that would otherwise have held the galley. The vessel was overwhelmed by the raging seas and the body of the prince was later washed up on the opposite shore of Jura and buried there in a cave.

West of Jura lies the island of Islay, a large island which, although not quite accurately, the old folk used to say was smaller than Mull by the area of a deer's sleeping space.

Off Luing lie the tiny Garvelloch Islands, or Isles of the Sea. The most southerly of the group has the ruins of a very early Christian church and settlement associated with St Brendan, which may even have been the first such establishment in Scotland. On the most northerly is an old dun supposed to have had connections with the rulers of Dalriada. St Columba first set foot in Scotland after his voluntary banishment from Ireland on the little island of Oronsay, adjacent to well-known Colonsay, which lies more to the south. However, since from there Columba could still faintly discern the distant coast of Ireland, he moved on to Iona, from which the Irish coast could no longer be seen.

Back on the Lochgilphead road and moving on for seven miles we come to Kilmelford by the new road that now runs above, instead of through, the pictureseque pass. Twelve miles further on we see Carnasserie Castle standing high above the west side of the road. This was latterly a Campbell stronghold, which was destroyed in 1685 as a punishment for that clan's earlier opposition to the Scottish Crown. The castle was the seat of the last Bishop of the Isles and Abbot of Iona, who was the author of the first book to be printed in the Gaelic language, a translation of *Liturgy* by John Knox.

At this point a road to the left leads to Ford at the south end of Loch Awe, from where two roads branch north, one following the east side of Loch Awe to Cladich, where it meets the Inveraray-Dalmally road already described; the other, skirting the west shore by Dalavich and the extensive forestry plantations, and passing through Taychreggan, one of the angling centres around the loch, finally meets the Oban road at Taynuilt.

Near the Ford end of the loch stands the old chapel of Killimeuer. An early account of its building narrates that the stones were cut and shaped in a quarry at Killevin, near Crarae, on Loch Fyne, ten miles as the crow flies across the hills. Then when all was prepared, volunteers formed a human chain along which the stones were passed from hand to hand until they were all positioned, each stone in its place, in the chapel building.

Loch Awe has more than its share of castles, apart from massive Kilchuirn. It is the heart of the lands of the Campbells, for once they had established their superiority over such clans as the MacGregors, MacDonalds and MacNaughtons from the 15th century onwards, their warcry 'It's a far cry to Lochow!' flaunted their impregnable hold which no enemy could penetrate.

The islands, which lie towards the wider, northern end of Loch Awe, have such lovely names as Innishail, Fraoch Eilean, Innis Chonnan, Innis Chonaill. On Fraoch Eilean stands a ruined castle that goes back to the days of Alexander III. Ardchonnel Castle, on Innis Chonaill, was one of the most important Campbell forts. Fincharn, one of the oldest, stands above the shore not far from Ford. Innishail was a sacred island with a very old Celtic nunnery, and was a place of interment for the clans round about.

Loch Awe is now ringed by many good hotels catering for the annual influx of anglers, with boats available for sightseeing as well as for fishermen.

From Carnasserie Castle we continue south on the Lochgilphead road into a district settled by even older races than the Scots, where the later Christian faith became firmly established. In the churchyard of the village of Kilmartin there is on display a fine collection of well-preserved, sculptured stones. Before leaving this district we should refer back to Loch Craignish, which lies between Loch Melford and Carnasserie Castle. A side road to the right skirting the north side of the loch takes us to Craignish Castle, originally built by the MacEacherns but later taken over by the Campbells. During the Wars of Montrose it defied a siege by the fierce Irish contingent of the Royalist forces under their leader Colkitto (Left-handed Coll).

Between Kilmartin and the Crinan Canal (which is the southern limit of our exploration) there is a level plain called the Moine Mhor, or Great Moss. Here there are duns, cup-marked rocks and other antiquities; but just a few hundred yards from the main road most impressive of all is the fortress-hill of Dunadd which rises like a great isolated rock to a height of 160 feet. This is one of the many items fully described in the guide book issued by the Scottish Development Department who are in charge of the place.

Traditionally, Dunadd was the first capital of Dalriada, to which King Fergus brought from Ireland the Stone of Destiny, the Lia Fail, Jacob's Pillow at Bethel. The first incomers had no easy establishment here. Little is known of its history before the eighth century, but around then it was attacked by the Picts, who held it for a time. What impresses the viewer are certain symbols inscribed on the flat surface of the rock at its highest point. There is the print of a human foot, the outline of a boar (now protected under glass) and a small bowl-shaped hollow. It is thought that here the Kings of Dalriada were crowned, with a foot in the imprint, anointed with holy oil or water from the rocky bowl, over the symbol of the sacred wild boar, thus taking the oath of kingship.

There are two similar but smaller footprints incised in a rock at Kilmichael, a mile or two to the east, which may have had some connection with the crowning of queens, perhaps in an earlier age when chiefship descended through the female instead of as later the male line.

We reach the Crinan Canal at Cairnbaan, about four miles from Lochgilphead. The canal, much used today by fishing craft and yachtsmen, runs for nine miles from Ardrishaig, on Loch Fyne four miles south of Lochgilphead, to Crinan on Loch Crinan, which opens on to the Firth of Lorne. It rises to a height of 64 feet above sea level by means of fifteen locks. The canal project was entered into prematurely to help the fishing fleets during a period of recession. It was designed by John Rennie and started in 1793 using private capital raised by private landowners. However, the Government had to step in with financial support before it was completed, but not without repeated delays.

It was finally opened in 1817. It allowed small ships to avoid the long exposed trip of over 100 miles round the Mull of Kintyre, that great headland that stretches south from the peninsula of Kintyre. Perhaps a more ambitious scheme would have been more successful if it had awaited the developing age of steamships, for the numerous locks lead to long delays in completing the passage of the canal. As in the case of Tarbet, Loch Lomond, here, too, the Viking galley, with Magnus Barefoot at the tiller — or steering oar, rather, for the rudder was a later invention in the Hebridean galley — was dragged overland on rollers, thus claiming that as a ship could sail round Kintyre, the area became a Viking possession.

Duntroon Castle stands commandingly on the north shore of Loch Crinan. It is supposed to be haunted by the ghost of a piper. This man, the story goes, had been captured and imprisoned in an upper storey of the castle. Now, he knew that his chief, with a fleet of galleys, was approaching to storm the castle, but the defenders, also well aware of this, had made the place impregnable; therefore the attackers would face annihilation. By playing a particular tune on his set of bagpipes the piper was able to warn his approaching kinsmen — 'Do not attack the castle' — whereupon they wisely withdrew. When the defenders realised how their well-laid plan had been foiled by the action of the piper they dragged him out of the chamber and cut off his fingers, a mutilation which led to his death. He was buried under a flat stone in the kitchen floor.

Lochgilphead is now reached, a neat little town at the head of Loch Gilp, an inlet of Loch Fyne. Our complete circuit of Loch Awe and the district can be closed by continuing to Inveraray, 24 miles distant. There are three interesting places about halfway along this stretch of road. The first is at Crarae, where the 50-acre policies of Crarae House have been converted into woodland gardens containing great masses of rhododendrons and azaleas, and many exotic species brought from all over the world. One attractive feature of the place is the glen, down which a burn of clear water descends in many cataracts. It is approached by woodland paths and is crossed by several little bridges. Another attractive feature is the grouping of the exhibits. Crarae is one of the most picturesque of Scotland's many show gardens. At the entrance to the gardens there is a Neolithic chambered cairn.

Furnace, a small industrial township, is the second place of interest. It lies beside the famous granite quarry of Dun Leacainn, which was first worked before the middle of last century. A quarry was also worked at Crarae, probably the one mentioned earlier in connection with the building of the chapel over near Ford. Like Bonawe quarry on Loch Etive, that at Furnace produces materials for roadworks. Before the start of quarrying, iron smelting was carried on here with imported Lancashire ore. As in the case of many other such centres, a great deal of local timber was cut down to make charcoal for the smelting processes; and when that industry ended, timber was still being felled for the manufacture of gunpowder, much of which was used in the quarries.

Thirdly, about five miles beyond Furnace we come to the show village of Auchindrain. In former times this was an important centre for the various trades connected with farming in what was then an extensive agricultural community; but times change, the village was abandoned and the houses became ruins. However, its restoration became a project of the Scottish Country Life Museum Trust in 1963, and since then Auchindrain has been transformed into a showplace, a museum not only of forgotten Scottish crafts, but also of the different styles and construction of houses connected with farming, as well as of tools and implements of the eighteenth and nineteenth centuries — a complete record of how an agricultural community used to live. It attracts large numbers of visitors, for whom all modern amenities are also provided.

This brings us back again to Inveraray by this section of the Glasgow to Campbeltown road from Lochgilphead, and we return to Dalmally and Oban.

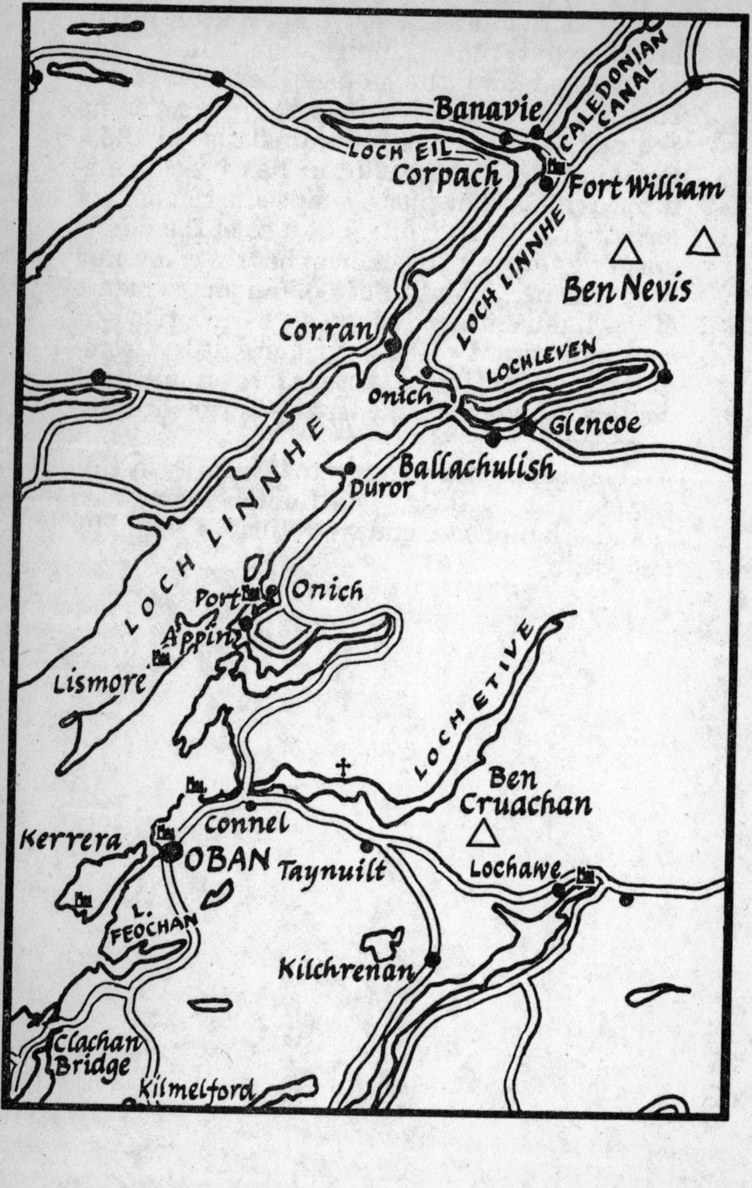

Banavie
CALEDONIAN CANAL
LOCH EIL
Corpach
Fort William
LOCH LINNHE
Ben Nevis
Corran
LOCHLEVEN
Onich
Glencoe
Ballachulish
Duror
LOCH LINNHE
Port
Onich
Appin
Lismore
LOCH ETIVE
Ben Cruachan
Connel
Kerrera
OBAN
Taynuilt
Lochawe
L. FEOCHAN
Kilchrenan
Clachan Bridge
Kilmelford

Oban to Fort William (49 miles)

A SCENIC COASTAL ROAD THAT becomes more spectacular the further north we go connects Oban and Fort William. From Oban we retrace our journey to Connel Ferry, where the road to the north swings to the right and crosses the former railway bridge with the Falls of Lora below. Just across the bridge is the flat fertile area known as the Moss of Achnacrae, where the road passes along the east side of Loch Nell past the scattered villages of Ledaig. Side roads to the right lead along the north side of Loch Etive to Ardchattan, which has been mentioned earlier. Loch Nell Castle stands at a northern inlet of the bay, and across the isthmus, on the south shore of Loch Creran, is Barcaldine Castle.

Of particular interest to archaeologists is the alleged site of ancient Beregonium, seat of the Pictish monarchy, on a small green hill just north of Ledaig. There are traces of a vitrified fort and several defensive positions or duns, much overgrown with whins and brambles. The name Beregonium may have been based on the old name of *Barr na Gobhann*, Ridge of the Smiths.

Barcaldine is another fertile area now given over to forestry plantations. During World War II the Ministry of Supply set up a factory here which was later taken over by Alginate Industries, of Girvan, Ayrshire, for the processing of seaweed. At one time it employed 50 or 60 workers, but like so many other concerns its operations have been affected by the present trade depression.

There is also an oyster hatchery here, one of a number of such experiments along the west coast.

Before leaving the topic of modern alginates, it is interesting to review the same theme in the context of the Napoleonic Wars, the kelp industry that flourished along the whole west coast for a few years, and the impact it had on the economy and social life. When imports of barilla, or soda ash, were no longer obtainable from the Continent, kelp ash, produced by burning dried kelps, came into its own as a effective substitute and was used extensively in such processes as glass-making and the bleaching of linen. Kelp, the 'Tangle of the Isles' (as it is romantically called), is that species of laminaria whose wide fronds, on their long rubbery stems, are seen swaying in great beds off rocky shores at low tide. It was gathered, dried in layers above highwater mark and burned, the resultant ash being collected and sent to the south. It brought tens of thousands of pounds in hard cash to the landowners at the expense of hard gruelling work by the coastal tenants, whole families of whom cut it, dragged it ashore, collected it in creels, and carried it up on their backs — or if lucky on the backs of ponies — to the burning sites. It is said that the incidence of rheumatism among the coastal communities was never worse than during the kelp boom. The industry came to an end when the Napoleonic wars were over and the higher quality barilla could again be imported; much to the chagrin and embarrassment of the local landowners, who had been collecting from £15 to £25 per ton and had come to depend on it for an income.

It may be added that this drying-up of easy money was a contributory factor in the gathering momentum of the Clearances, whose effects in the Highlands you will see in the ruined villages and deserted homesteads. Easier communications, education, and ready cash had allowed many of the landed class to indulge themselves as never before in the sophisticated society of the South. When they lost the income from kelp they began to raise rents in a desperate effort to obtain cash to maintain their new lifestyle; but rents became so high and hard cash so scarce among the tenants that they could hardly be paid. Incoming sheep farmers, however, were more than willing to pay even higher rents for land converted to sheep farms, with the result that the original tenants were evicted and sheep installed.

This digression has taken us far from the Fort William road, which we follow round Loch Creran and by Appin. At the old church here a side road turns left for Port Appin, from which there is the shortest ferry crossing to the fertile, ten-mile long island of Lismore, whose name, *Lios Mor*, means the Great Enclosure, where St Moluag's monastery once stood and which for a time was also the seat of the Bishops of Argyll. The main ferry to the island runs from Oban.

Sometimes Lismore is called the Great Garden, since unlike the predominating acid barren volcanic rocks of the surrounding districts, its limestone rocks make it green and fertile. On Lismore are the old castles of Tirefoor and Coeffin. An island of ancient traditions, it is held to have been a place of interment for the Pictish Royal Family.

Portnacroish, a mile further on, has associations with the Appin murder which will be mentioned later. There, quite near the shore, on an islet in Loch Laich (an inlet of Loch Linnhe) stands Stalker Castle, now restored as a dwelling-place. It was built by Duncan Stewart of Appin as a residence for James IV during his hunting excursions, and Duncan was appointed custodian. The name Stalker comes from *Stalcaire*, a Gaelic word meaning a deer hunter.

The road hugs the coastline for the next six miles to Duror, then turns inland for two miles until it reaches the shore again near the entrance to Loch Leven. It then goes round the base of the Glenduror Forest with the twin peaks of Ben Vair high above, Sgorr Dhonuill (3284ft) and Sgorr Dhearg (3302ft), to reach the township of Ballachulish — 'The Town by the Narrows'. Until recently this was a dreary north-facing village among the scars and rubble of the disused slate quarries, once a thriving industry that was started in 1761. However, the village is having a complete face-lift; scars are being landscaped and the whole environment transformed, and already Ballachulish is becoming an attractive little place.

Just before we arrive at the town we come to the new bridge across the narrows of Loch Leven and join the main road for the remaining 13 miles to Fort William.

Before passing on to the next stage of our exploration, and as we stand beside the new bridge, it might be interesting to recall the Appin Murder and how, a fact that is little known, the aftermath of the incident is connected with the life of our great missionary-explorer David Livingstone.

As you look up at the south end of the bridge you will see a high bluff above you to the left, above the hotel on the lower road. On the top you will notice a simple square monument with an explanatory panel, surmounted by a large rounded block of white quartz which is visible from some distance around, although becoming somewhat hidden by scrub growth. The monument is reached by a flight of steps from the end of the bridge and it stands on the spot where James Stewart, James of the Glen, was hanged on 7 November 1752 for a crime he did not commit.

After the Jacobite uprising in 1745/6 the estates of many sympathisers were forfeited and they fled abroad to avoid retribution. Factors were appointed by the Commissioners to manage the estates in their absence, and those men were most unpopular in the eyes of Jacobite sympathisers. One such factor was Colin Campbell of Glenure, who was known as the Red Fox. However, he does not appear to have been an unduly harsh man, although he made a number of enemies. In fact, he had a distant connection by marriage with James Stewart, in whose case he was reported to have been lenient to a point where he was reproved by the Commissioners.

In May 1752, Campbell of Glenure and a servant were following the path through the nearby Wood of Lettermore when they were ambushed and Campbell was shot by an assailant who vanished among the trees. The unfortunate man expired almost at once. The name of the man who fired the shot was never revealed, although it appears to have been a secret kept by a local family and handed down from one generation to another. As no likely culprit could be found, James Stewart, who lived at Duror, near the estate of Stewart of Ardshiel that was factored by the Red Fox, was apprehended.

Stoutly protesting his innocence, in fact having been away from the district on the day of the crime, he was conveyed to Inveraray. It is said that the real murderer was so overcome by this miscarriage of justice that he had to be forcibly confined to the house to avoid his coming forward and confessing: nor would James Stewart allow him to do so (word had got through to him secretly) for he was so optimistic about his own release. Alas for his hopes. Before a prejudiced Campbell court and judge he was convicted and sentenced to be hanged near the scene of the crime. As a warning to the people the body was left hanging under a military guard, until by 1756 only the bones, wired together as they fell apart, swung from the gibbet.

Disgusted by this unchristian degradation of a brave man, three brothers from a local Livingstone family, Neil Mor (or Big), Donald and John planned to remove the remains and give them decent burial. So late one evening John fell into conversation with the bored sentry and invited him to come down to the inn for a drink. Nothing loth, the soldier left his post — surely, he thought, no-one would grudge him a few minutes' absence from his monotonous job;

whereupon the other two brothers, who had been watching, hurried from their place of concealment, reverently took down the bones from the gibbet and carried them, together with the gibbet itself, down to a rowing boat they had drawn up on the shore below. A stiff tide prevented them from landing on the traditional burial island of St Munde, but they did so on an adjacent islet and interred the bones there. The gibbet they threw into the sea, which washed it up first at Rudha na Croich (Point of the Gibbet), and finally at Portnacroish, where it lay for a long time shunned by the people.

Fearing retribution after flouting the authorities so boldly, Neil Mor and Donald rowed first to Morvern, but being still too close to the scene they moved on to Mull and settled as respected crofters on the island of Ulva, off the west of Mull. In 1792 Neil Mor and his family moved to Glasgow, then to Blantyre, where his son Neil Bheag (Small) married Agnes Hunter. Their second son, Neil Mor's grandson, David Livingstone, who was to become one of the nation's great explorers, was born there on 19 March 1813. His life was a tribute to the bravery and loyal traditions of his forefathers.

Fort William
Aonach Beag
Ben Nevis
LOCH LINNHE
LOCHLEVEN
Kinlochleven
Onich
Glencoe
BLACKWATER RESR.
Ballachulish
GLEN COE
RANNOCH MOOR
The Three Sisters
Buachaille Etive Mor
Black Mount
LOCH ETIVE
LOCH LYON
Bridge of Orchy
Beinn Dorain
Ben Cruachan
Tyndrum
Ben Lui
Crianlarich
Ben More
Ben Vorlich
LOCH SLOY
Arrochar
Tarbet

Tyndrum to Fort William by Glencoe (47 miles)

FORT WILLIAM, 103 MILES FROM Glasgow, is reached by the A82 route from the south which has already been described as far as Tyndrum. Here it forks to the right, leaving the Oban road, and curves up to the southern extension of the Moor of Rannoch, crossing the watershed (the county boundary between Argyll and Perthshire) at 1033 feet in the narrow glen between Ben Odhar (2948ft) and the lesser Beinn Bheag (2149ft). From this point it is downhill to Bridge of Orchy. It is a splendid well-graded motor road, completed in 1935, through a lonely land of wide horizons, bogs and lochs, rimmed by high mountain peaks. The stranger is both awed and fascinated by the scale and desolation of the landscape.

From Bridge of Orchy a narrow side road runs south-west for 14 miles to connect with the Oban road near Dalmally. The pools, falls, and rock structures of the River Orchy, another good salmon river, make it one of the most photogenic in Scotland, especially at such spots as the Goat Pool, Witches' Pool and Canal Pool halfway along the glen.

About five miles from Tyndrum the slope of Ben Doirean rises in one unbroken symmetrical sweep from the valley floor to the summit cairn 3524 feet above. One can understand how this mountain inspired the poet Duncan Ban Macintyre to compose his great Gaelic poem *In Praise of Ben Doirean.* About four miles from this point you will see the ruins of his home at Druimliart, beside Inveroran, which lies on the old road to Glencoe on the west side of Loch Tulla. The old road is included now as a section of what is called the new West Way, a track designed for hikers, starting at Loch Lomond and heading for Fort William, avoiding main roads wherever possible. The old Glencoe road forms an ideal link in this route.

Like the railway across the Moor of Rannoch, the new road is a triumph of engineering. In parts it had to cross soft peat bogs over 20 feet deep, impracticable to excavate and fill in. Instead the engineers sank huge rafts of brushwood and branches over which road and railway were laid. Standing beside one of these sections of the road when a heavy vehicle passes, one can feel the slight springiness of the road surface. Peat has a remarkable neutral chemical action whereby organic matter buried in it is preserved almost indefinitely. Strange finds sometimes turn up in the peat, from clothing and equipment of the past, even bodies, to kegs of 'bog butter' (more common in Ireland), where a summer surplus of butter was stored in kegs and dug into the peat as a form of larder where it would be preserved for use in the winter, and its location forgotten or lost.

The bogs hold massive roots of the ancient Caledonian Forest, now vanished except for a few stray patches, one of which is to be seen west of Loch Tulla. During the road construction here for years the sides were heaped with the bleaching skeletons of old roots and trunks excavated from the road bed.

Even the signs along the road at the various summits convey that sense of loneliness: Rannoch Moor, Black Mount, and Carn nam Bocan, all over 1000 feet above sea level, with Black Mount the highest at 1143 feet. Carn nam Bocan (Cairn of Ghosts) is situated appropriately enough where the road leaves Rannoch Moor and begins to descend Glen Coe. However, surprisingly enough, the Moor is alive with bird life in spring and summer.

Before we move on to the west, mention should be made of the railway, the old West Highland line from Glasgow to Fort William and Mallaig, which has paralleled the road all the way from Loch Lomond. At Loch Tulla it swings away to the east of the Moor to Rannoch Station, passing at Corrour siding one of the most remote places in the British railway system. Rannoch station connects by road with all the roads in the Grampian Region, although only a very tenuous track, a footpath by bogs and lochans, connects the Glencoe road at Kingshouse Inn with the station. It is difficult to visualise mounted troops combing this moor with its treacherous surface in search of the fugitives, as described by Stevenson in *Kidnapped*.

We have now turned westwards towards the mountain masses of the Black Mount and Glencoe, whose corries hold snow beds until early summer. On the right on a loop of the old road we come to the first habitation since leaving Loch Tulla, Kingshouse Inn. Today it is a well-known centre for climbers, ski-ers and explorers of the hills. The first ski-tow and chair lift in Britain was constructed here in 1955, starting beside the main road not far from the Inn and conveying afficionados and sightseers to the upper slopes and snow beds of that nest of 'Munroes' called the Black Mount, with such mountains as Meall a'Bhuiridh, Mam Choire Easain, and many others with names no easier on the Lowland tongue.

An inn has stood here for hundreds of years, a meeting-place for drovers in the old days, billets for soldiers in the unsettled times and mentioned by Stevenson in *Kidnapped.* In 1792 Colonel Hamilton was stationed here with a large body of soldiers to search for and exterminate survivors from the Glencoe Massacre. However, he arrived too late, and the weather was against him; so he had to confine his activities to looting, burning the houses and driving off all the livestock of the unfortunate MacDonalds of Glencoe to the garrison at Fort William.

A mile west of the inn, Buchaille Etive Mor (the Big Shepherd of Etive) towers up to a height of 3345 feet. The rock faces and chimneys of its eastern faces, and the Crowberry Ridge — the tower standing out boldly on the summit — are some of the best-known climbs in Britain, presenting a challenge to experienced climbers, several of whom over the years sadly have fallen victim to the exacting standards of the mountain.

A mile further along the road, to the right, is the dwelling of Altnafeadh, from which a signposted track leads north across the ridge of Aonach Eagach (Notched Ridge) and down the other side to Kinlochleven. Until 1750 this was a gruelling six-mile stretch of drove road, but it was reconstructed into a very rough military road as a short cut to Kinlochleven and through the Mamore glens to Fort William. It became known as the 'Devil's Staircase'. Under winter conditions it was a cruel track, and indeed in 1909 when the aluminium smelting works were being built at Kinlochleven, using water power from the Blackwater Reservoir a few miles to the east, many jobless labourers seeking employment tramped all the way from the south, taking the short cut across the Devil's Staircase. Some died from exhaustion and exposure and their bodies were found up here when the snows melted.

Between Kingshouse Inn and the Great Shepherd a narrow side road leads through the glen to the head of Glen Etive and the loch, past the lovely hill slopes beloved by the legendary Deirdre.

Now the mountains close in on either side, and before us Glen Coe descends for five miles from Altnafeadh to the sea at Loch Leven. This is undoubtedly the most magnificent, saddest, and best-known glen in Scotland. Rearing up to the left are the vertical buttresses of the mountains known as the 'Three Sisters', with the dark opening of Ossian's Cave on the face of Aonach Dubh — a romantic name for a cave impracticable of approach and useless for occupancy. This particular 'Sister' has some of the stiffest rock-face climbing in the country, and between the first and second of the trio the 'Lost Valley' lies high up towards the skyline. All this is backed up by peak over peak, with a glimpse of all the top of Bidean nam Beann (3766ft), the highest mountain in Argyll. It is a dangerous area for inexperienced climbers. On the northern side of the glen Aonach Eagach curves in a long high saw-toothed ridge, a scramble of four miles or more for the energetic.

Near the head of the glen the old road again diverges to the right at a higher level, passing a square rocky spur which used to be negotiated in hairpin bends on a gradient of 1 in 4. This is known as the 'Study', a word meaning 'Anvil' in both Lowland Scots and the translated Gaelic name, and is sometimes referred to as the 'Anvil of the Mists'. The great square rock does resemble an anvil when seen from below. It is well worth walking up this short section of the old road to see the arresting view from the Study. To complete the picture of Highland grandeur, the River Coe tumbles down in a series of cataracts, with one particular waterfall lying just below a rock cutting and parking area beside the new road just below the Study. The Coe flows down into Loch Triochatan, beyond which the glen flattens out and opens to the north-west, where Carnoch, the modern Glencoe village, lies beside Loch Leven.

Beyond Loch Triochatan the old road again branches off to the right, passing Clachaig Inn and the nearby Signal Rock, from which the signal to commence the infamous massacre is said to have been given. It passes the pathetic traces of the razed hamlet and the monument to the memory of the massacred MacDonalds, before rejoining the new road at the sea.

Here are the facts of this tragic story of perfidy, spite and murder, sponsored by some of the most powerful people in the land. The clan chiefs had been ordered to swear allegiance to King William III before 1 January 1692, but most of the Highland chiefs still owed their allegiance to James II, who although fleeing from the throne of Britain was still the true king in the direct line according to the old clan traditions. Therefore the presence of what they regarded as a foreign king was much resented.

The first MacDonalds of Glencoe — MacIan, they were called — had as their first chief a son of Angus Og, Lord of the Isles. In 1692 the old chief deferred the hated action of swearing this new allegiance for as long as he could, but in the end he rode to Fort William to take the oath. Colonel Hill there told him he was not empowered to act, and directed MacDonald to Inveraray, where he would have to go before Sir Colin Campbell of Ardkinglas, the Sheriff there. Delayed by snowstorms the old chief arrived at Inveraray one day late — which gave the authorities the excuse for later events. The Sheriff was absent and the Oath could not be accepted until 6 January, but MacIan returned home at last much relieved at having completed the formality.

However, towards the end of January a party of over 100 soldiers of the Earl of Argyll's Regiment, led by Captain Campbell of Glenlyon, came into Glencoe. There was no love lost between the MacDonalds and the Glenlyon, for on one occasion the clansmen had cleared Glenlyon of its cattle. When challenged by the MacDonalds, Glenlyon explained that his party sought billets with the Glencoe people, as the fort at Fort William was overcrowded: further he gave his word of honour that not a hand would be raised against the MacDonalds. Afer a fortnight had passed, suspicions were allayed and both the soldiers and the folk of the glen were fraternising freely.

Then came the deed of treachery that incensed the whole country; even to this day the name of Campbell is an anathema to the older people in Glencoe. Glenlyon received a letter from Colonel Hamilton ordering him bluntly to carry out a wholesale extermination of the 'rebells' in Glencoe, to begin at 5 am the following day, 13 February 1692. No-one was to be spared, and to ensure this, hill passes, ferries and boats on the loch were to be guarded by soldiers. The Government was 'not to be troubled with prisoners'. Several of the soldiers were so appalled by the terms of their orders that they dropped hints to a few of the MacDonalds, notably the chief's two sons, which allowed them to escape in time although the old chief himself, an honourable and courageous man in his age, firmly refused to believe there was any evil intent. He was one of the 38 clansmen murdered in their beds or in their houses. Many did manage to escape, but nearly 80 died in the snows and bitter winter cold of the hills. However, the majority of the people were saved by that same weather which held up the converging ring of troops.

One or two of the soldiers avoided the actual killing as best they could and there were a few humane incidents, such as the case of one soldier who, when ordered to seek out and kill a baby heard crying, returned to his officer showing him on his bayonet the blood of a dog he had killed instead. It is true that the soldiers were acting under direct military orders; to have refused would have meant the firing squad for disobedience. What condemned them in the eyes of the country was rather what followed, the debauchery, murder, rape and killing of a trusting community, men, women and children alike, who had welcomed the soldiers as friends.

However, the true blame for ordering the massacre goes far up the social and political scale, in fact, to King William himself, even if he was unaware of the order he was signing. This order was the outcome of the spite and malevolence of the then Secretary of State for Scotland, Dalrymple, Master of Stair, against the Highlanders. Weeks before the Massacre he had stated in writing to Sir Thomas Livingstone that he hoped the clans in Lochaber would be destroyed by the troops. He later expressed his disappointment that the Camerons and others had taken the Oath in time, and added his vindictive pleasure in having as an excuse for exterminating the MacDonalds of Glencoe the fact that MacIan had failed to record his submission in time, the reason for the delay having been withheld. This followed a discussion with Campbell of Breadalbane who entirely agreed. This action came near to precipitating a fresh rising by the Highland clans.

For a long time there was this contempt held against Highlanders by people of the South. A hundred years after the Massacre, for instance, William Pitt, Prime Minister, is quoted as having said — 'I have found a new use for Highlanders; they make good cannon fodder'.

But leaving behind these gloomy memories, we proceed to the salty tides running along the narrows of Loch Leven up to Kinlochleven, eight miles away at the head of the loch. In Gaelic *Kin* or *Ceann* means 'Head', a word we frequently come across. At the mouth of Glen Coe we have two choices of route, to the left for the main road past Ballachulish crossing the new bridge built in 1975 to replace the former ferry, or to the right for the more leisurely and scenically-rewarding sixteen-mile circuit of Loch Leven. In the second case, the road along the south side passes below the Pap of Glencoe

(2430ft) rising high above the loch and gives spectacular views from the high points, especially of the mountains of the Mamore Forest and the Ben Nevis massif. This road was reconstructed by prisoners of war during the 1914-18 war. Passing through the semi-industrialised township of Kinlochleven, shut in at the head of the loch among high hills, we continue along the north side following more closely to the shore until we meet the Ballachulish road at the north end of the bridge. From Kinlochleven tracks run through the connecting glens to Glen Nevis and Fort William; wonderful hill walking. On the Mamore section motor-cycle reliability trials are held at least once a year, to the disgust of dedicated hill walkers.

Looking across the loch towards Glen Coe we see the island of Eilean Munde, called after the Celtic Saint Mun. For centuries this has been used as a burial ground, and here most of the victims of the Glencoe Massacre were interred.

North Ballachulish and Onich are sunny places catering for a considerable tourist trade, with hotels and accommodation. The road now turns north along Loch Linnhe, passing Corran Ferry (for Morvern and Ardnamurchan) in the remaining eight miles to Fort William. Strangers coming south in the old days have been known to mistake Corran for Ballachulish Ferry: crossing to Ardgour, with many a weary mile to Ardnamurchan, where the road ends, would be a frustrating experience for the man hurrying south! In fact we think a notice once stood here that read 'This is NOT Ballachulish Ferry!' Along the 'Golden Mile' now, past crofts and tourist accommodation, we come at last to Fort William.

Fort William

THE TOWN OF FORT WILLIAM STANDS almost at the head of Loch Linnhe, where many roads converge. At this strategic centre a fort was first built in 1665 by General Monk to keep the restless clans in the district in order. It was a structure of earth sited at the north end of what now is the town. This was replaced by stonework in the time of King William III and in his honour the name of the place was changed from Maryburgh to Fort William. Its military history goes back beyond the eighth century, for in those early times a dun or fort stood where the later Inverlochy Castle was built, two miles north of the town where the River Lochy flows into the sea. A treaty was signed here between Achaius, who became King of Dalriada in 787, and the King of France.

Two important battles were fought here at Inverlochy, the first in the early 15th century in the days of the Lords of the Isles, when Donald Balloch and his Islesmen, disputing the succession to the Crown of Scotland, utterly defeated a much larger Royal army, although with little concrete result. Better known is the second Battle of Inverlochy fought on 31 January 1645 between on one side the Duke of Argyll and his Covenanting force of Campbell followers supported by a large Lowland contingent, and on the other Montrose, with his Highland army of 1800, including the Irish contingent under Colkitto. Neil Munro's *John Splendid* describes the night march undertaken by Montrose's men under dreadful winter conditions over the 2500-foot Corriearrick Pass, which allowed a surprise morning attack on the army of Argyll which was completely routed, although some early resistance was shown. Argyll himself escaped in his galley leaving the troops to their fate. Thanks to the humanity of his brave opponent a massacre was avoided.

Today Fort William, like Oban, is a popular bustling tourist centre which is about to be greatly developed, with its many hotels and guest houses catering for a large annual influx of visitors. Perhaps among its many amenities the West Highland Museum is outstanding, with its relics of Prince Charles Edward Stuart ('Bonnie Prince Charlie') with whom the district to the west is particularly associated. Like Oban, Fort William has a distillery, but in addition it has some modern industrialisation. North-east of the town are the aluminium works and electricity generating station powered by water conducted by an underground tunnel passing under Ben Nevis from Loch Treig, 15 miles away, and also by water from Loch Laggan on the road to Newtonmore. Fort William, with its electricity first generated in 1896 in this Lochaber Power Scheme, was one of the first towns in Britain to be lit by electricity. There is also a training centre, using the deep waters of the sea lochs, for deep-sea divers, particularly for the North Sea oil developments. Over 100 men are based here.

During the unsettled times military roads radiated from here, the most important being Wade's Road, whose line is closely followed today as far as Fort Augustus by the main Inverness road. The road westwards to Arisaig was built by Telford in 1800-1804. The West Highland Railway from Glasgow reached Fort William in 1894 and was later extended to Mallaig: thus many private and commercial interests are served.

Lying as it does almost in the shadow of Britain's highest mountain, Ben Nevis (4406ft), Fort William is a major centre for climbers, hikers, and lovers of the hills and glens. Yachtsmen gather here, at the point where Loch Linnhe opens south into the maze of sea lochs, and just to the north, the Caledonian Canal offers a short cut along the Great Glen to the waters of the Moray Firth at Inverness.

While it is not true that all Fort William people lean forward through constantly climbing Ben Nevis, the ascent of this mountain attracts great numbers of visitors. The rounded mass of the Ben is by no means impressive from a distance; it is only when on the hill itself, or when it is viewed from neighbouring peaks, that its true scale and impressiveness show up, especially the two-mile long range of stupendous cliffs on the north side where snow usually lies throughout the year.

The summit is a place of sudden and unpredictable changes of weather. It can be reached by a slogging walk up a well-defined path that begins at Achentee Farm in Glen Nevis. The track is much as it was in the days of early motor cars, when a Model 'T' Ford car managed to complete the ascent under its own steam, so to speak, after some amateur road building at the acute bends, the first of a number of such advertising efforts. There is the usual useful mountain indicator at the top. A thick-walled observatory was built here in 1883 by the Scottish Meteorological Society. It consisted of four rooms and took five months to build. In spite of its usefulness, however, the Government refused to pay the full cost of maintenance and it had to close down in 1904. It is now a ruin, as is also the hostel built there later and abandoned in 1915. The views from the summit are truly magnificent and in clear weather the immense sweep of colourful mountain peaks and lochs takes the breath away. The coast of Ireland can be seen 150 miles away and the great mass of the Cairngorms over to the east.

There is a wide choice of walks and climbs to suit all categories of mountain lovers, from the expert to the casual walker. Glen Nevis, for instance, offers a most attractive walk — or drive — for eight miles to the car park. It curves south and east from Fort William round the base of Ben Nevis which it divides from the Mamore Forest to the south, with paths branching off to Kinlochleven, Spean Bridge and elsewhere. So far its beauties have been preserved, although local authorities have been under pressure to have dams built across the glen. We should explain at this point that the word 'Forest', so often met with in Scotland in this context, is a misnomer. It comes from a Latin word 'Feris' meaning 'out at the door', literally, out of doors. A quotation given in the OED from F Pollock *Land Laws, v II, p 40, 1883,* probably sums it up best:

> The prescence of trees . . . is not required to make a forest in this sense. The great mark is the absence of enclosures.

We cannot emphasise too strongly the need for care and foresight when exploring the Scottish mountains. Thick mists can come down with deceptive speed, with dire results for the unprepared. Sudden hail and snow showers can develop in the late spring almost out of the blue. Never forget that even in midsummer the temperature at the top can be very different from that at the foot; it can fall 1°F for about every 300 feet of ascent. So use common sense and wear protective clothing and suitable footwear and carry rations and a compass. We recommend, too, a stout walking stick for the not so young. So many avoidable accidents have taken place through sheer inexperience that in this country we could well impose a charge for calling out search parties, medical teams, and even helicopter crews, and volunteers who have to sacrifice working hours.

With so much to see and do in and around Fort William, the newcomer is well-advised to contact the town's excellent Tourist Information Centre for guidance.

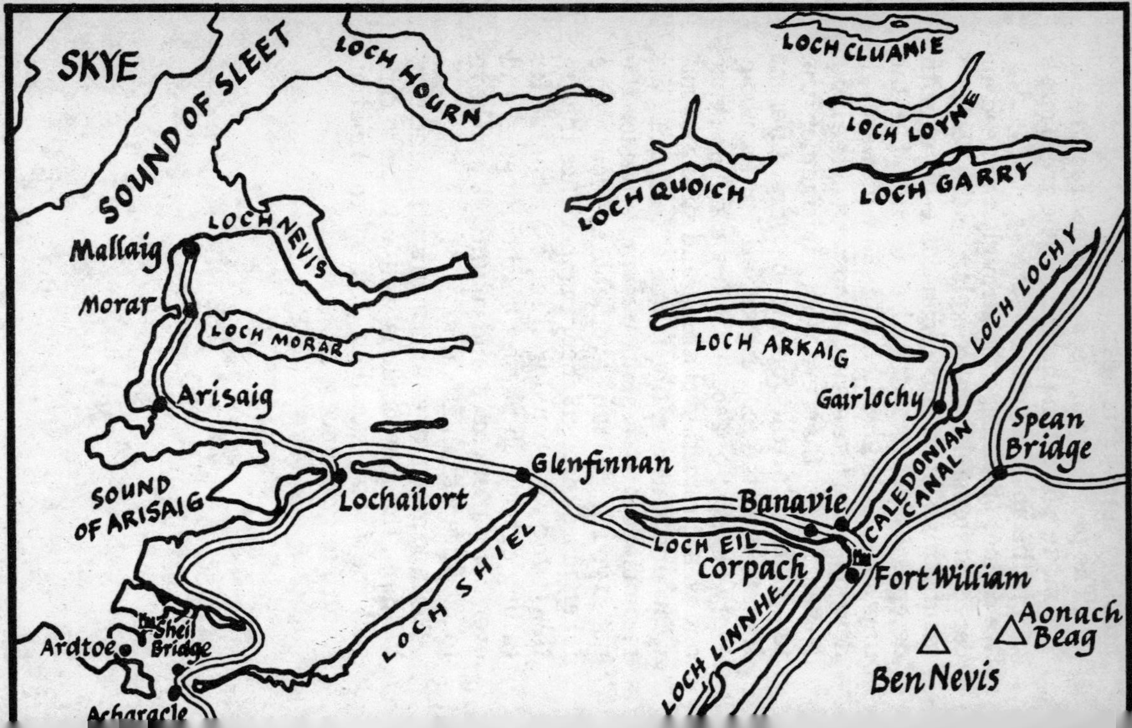
SKYE
SOUND OF SLEET
LOCH HOURN
LOCH CLUANIE
LOCH LOYNE
LOCH QUOICH
LOCH GARRY
LOCH NEVIS
Mallaig
Morar
LOCH MORAR
LOCH ARKAIG
LOCH LOCHY
Arisaig
Gairlochy
Spean Bridge
Glenfinnan
SOUND OF ARISAIG
Lochailort
Banavie
CALEDONIAN CANAL
LOCH EIL
Corpach
Fort William
LOCH SHIEL
Sheil Bridge
Ardtoe
Acharacle
LOCH LINNHE
Aonach Beag
Ben Nevis

Fort William to Mallaig (48 miles)

MANY ROADS CENTRE ON FORT WILLIAM which is on the main road to Inverness (66 miles) by the Great Glen and Loch Ness. Newtonmore, on the Perth-Inverness road, is 49 miles distant by Spean Bridge and Loch Laggan, and roads connect with the Inverness road at Glengarry and Glenmoriston for Loch Duich and Kyle of Lochalsh. By sea, Fort William used to be connected with Oban by regular MacBrayne sailings, now only sometimes by the occasional cruise up Loch Linnhe. Westwards from the town lies perhaps the most picturesque, romantic and historical district in the Highlands, through which runs one of the Roads to the Isles — famed in song — and also the scenic line of the West Highland Railway, which covers 48 miles from Lochaber, by Ardgour, Moidart, Arisaig and Morar to the road and rail terminus at Mallaig, with sea connections from there to Skye and the smaller Hebridean islands.

Before taking the road westwards round the head of Loch Linnhe, it is recommended that a diversion (8 miles) be made towards Spean Bridge, to explore the scenic configurations of Glen Roy, and after that the Cameron country between Loch Arkaig and Loch Lochy. At Spean Bridge turn right for a further four miles, then turn on to a side road to the left at Roy Bridge. Here, for miles along the upper hill slopes of Glen Roy, you will see the strange natural phenomenon called the Parallel Roads of Glen Roy, level 'roads' or platforms cut into the hill slopes at elevations of 1149 feet, 1068 feet and 851 feet. In the old days they were a source of wonder and folklore. However, the real reason for their presence is more prosaic. They were caused by erosion over a very long period of time at different stages of the last Ice Age by the waters of a lake whose levels dropped as the ice receded and in so doing uncovered new outlets. It was dammed back by the great glacier moving down Glen More past the mouth of Glen Roy.

Back at Spean Bridge, continue along the main road up the hill and fork left at the Commando Monument towards Achnacarry. Achnacarry is the home of the chief of the Clan Cameron, 'Locheil' as he is called. Destroyed by Cumberland as a punishment for Locheil's part in the '45 uprising, Achnacarry was rebuilt later on the same site. By the end of the 18th century the Government considered that their unremitting persecution of the clansmen had finally ended the Highland Problem. Forfeited estates were restored to many of the chiefs: but note that they, and not, as under the Clan System, the clan as a unit, were designated owners of the land, which gave them a free hand to deal with the estates.

The district round about figured much in the books by D K Broster such as *The Gleam in the*

North, *The Flight of the Heron* and *The Dark Mile*, all written about the Jacobite uprising. The Dark Mile, *Mile Dorcha* in the Gaelic, is a long avenue of close-set trees not far from Achnacarry. Seemingly, tree planting was being carried out when the call to arms came with the landing of Prince Charles Edward Stuart, and the remaining seedlings were hastily earthed in over this section. The whole district around Loch Arkaig, especially to the west, is closely associated with the wanderings of the fugitive Prince after Culloden. A path follows the edge of this loch by Glen Pean into the hills and glens leading over to the heads of Loch Morar and Loch Hourn, the 'Rough Bounds' as this district is called, one of the least frequented and most desolate parts of the Highlands.

Any reader of *The Lyon in Mourning* by Duncan Forbes, and its sequel *Account of Charge and Discharge* by Murray of Broughton (Prince Charlie's Paymaster) will be stirred to read of the personal courage and uncomplaining endurance of the Prince through all his misfortunes, although we cannot forget his lack of wisdom and practical experience in warfare, nor his forlorn ideals. Interest will be aroused by the description of the treasure of 30,000 golden Louis d'Or which arrived from France too late to help him in his campaign. You will read in the *Account* of how this treasure — less a bag containing 700 Louis d'Or, removed from a keg, the whole being too heavy to carry away by the three guards who defected — was carried from Achnacarry House by the two Cameron leaders and hidden nearby for greater security, all in the space of one dark night. What happened to it? Was it hidden in the waters of Loch Arkaig

. . . or in the bed of a watercourse? Is it still there? The time factor must have been so short that this heavy load could only have been hidden within a short radius. Or, as is said, did Murray of Broughton turn traitor in the end and secure the treasure for himself?

During the war Achnacarry House was a Commando training centre whose activities are well described in *Castle Commando* by Donald Gilchrist. The fine monument above Spean Bridge was erected to the memory of this vital unit.

The Camerons were among the fiercest of the Highland clans in the old days, and clansmen were famous for feats of individual strength. A story is told of one Cameron, known as the 'Strong Man of Lochaber', who lived not far from Spean Bridge. An old lady who used to live there vouched for the facts. One day as he was walking along he came across a crofter standing disconsolately beside his horse and cart which had slipped sideways into the ditch. The horse, exhausted by its vain efforts to move the cart, was lying down between the shafts. Taking in the scene the 'Strong Man' took off his jacket and handed it to the crofter. Then he went down, unyoked the horse, and dragged it back up to the road. Then getting down between the shafts he gripped and heaved until first one wheel, then the other, came free and with a great effort he dragged the cart bodily out of the ditch and back on to the road. As he retrieved his jacket and wiped his brow he remarked to the crofter:

> 'Indeed, I am not surprised that the poor horse could not move the cart: I had a big enough job myself!'

From here we return to Fort William, where the road crosses the River Lochy near the ruins of

Inverlochy Castle just short of Corpach. Not everyone knows the ancient associations of this name, which in translation means 'Place of Bodies'. When the sanctity of Iona was at its peak and kings and dignitaries sought interment in the holy soil of that island, Corpach was a place, a staging-place if you like, to which the bodies of the dead were conveyed, especially from the Inverness direction by the Great Glen, the most convenient route for the last journey of Norwegian kings who are interred in Iona. From here the dead were taken by galley down Loch Linnhe to Mull and Iona, sometimes sheltering during bad weather at the halfway islands of Colonsay or Oronsay, where there were Christian settlements. Some were landed on the eastern shore of Mull and carried overland to Iona Ferry.

At Corpach we see where the Caledonian Canal leaves Loch Linnhe at the start of a series of eight locks called Neptune's Staircase. There are 29 locks in all along the whole length of the canal (22 miles) although the total distance from Corpach to Inverness is just over 60 miles. Lochs Lochy, Oich and Ness are convenient links between the sections of the canal. The highest point, Loch Oich, is 106 feet above sea level. In the early years of the century MacBrayne's paddle steamer *Gondolier* used to sail regularly along the whole length of the canal. Now it is used by small vessels such as fishing vessels and yachts, to avoid the long stormy journey round the north of Scotland by Cape Wrath and the Pentland Firth. Construction of the canal was started in 1804 under Telford, but was held up by recurring troubles until 1822, when it opened for a time. Dogged by further problems it had to close, and was not reopened as a going concern until 1847. It is designed with a depth of 20 feet and a width of 50 feet, which will allow the passage of craft with a draught up to 14 feet.

In 1966 a £20 million pulp mill was opened at Corpach, giving employment to 2000 men and using both the products of forestry plantations and also imported cargoes. Ancillary industries, such as the manufacture of fine paper and a large sawmill followed. All waste, including dangerous chemicals, is burned and thus pollution of the loch is avoided. Unfortunately, at the time of writing the future of the project is very uncertain, and it will be a tragedy to such a comparatively remote community if this industry comes to an end.

Beyond Corpach road and rail hug the north shore of Loch Eil. Halfway along the shore you will come to Achdalieu, scene of an exploit during the wars of Montrose by young Sir Ewen Cameron of Locheil. Not all chiefs hastened to take the Oath of Allegiance to a new king — or in Locheil's case to the Commonwealth. The seeming stubborness of Highland Chiefs to take this Oath to acknowledge a new king goes deep into the traditional roots of the ancient Clan System, where Chiefs swore allegiance only to the man they held to be their true king in the direct line, hence their reluctance to accept the Commonwealth, or in Jacobite times, the House of Orange in place of the Stewart line, which they held to be the true and only line of descent.

Young Locheil — he was in his early 20s — not only refused to take the Oath, but with his Camerons became a strong unit in the army of Montrose. When not absent from his lands with his fighting men he conducted such successful guerrilla raids on the garrison at Fort William as to pin down a disproportionately high number of English troops. Food and supplies could only be brought in under a guard of 2-300 regular soldiers, and even then not without risk, for spies within the fort and observers on the hills around reported every movement.

One day a party of 300 sailed along Loch Eil to cut timber on Locheil's lands at Achdalieu, much to his wrath. With only a small party of Camerons he laid such a successful ambush at the landing point that the woodcutters and their guards had to fight their way back to the boats with severe casualties. The Highlanders even pursued them into the water and cut them down there. Against the loss of only five Camerons, a total of 138 redcoats were slain. This was one of the last occasions in the Highlands when bows and arrows were used to supplement firearms.

During the fight Locheil was confronted by a powerful English officer whom he disarmed, but who closed with him and they both fell into a dry watercourse with the officer on top. Neither could free himself to use his knife; but as the Englishman pushed himself up in an effort to do so, Locheil was able to fling an arm round the officer's neck and drag his head down until he could close his teeth in the exposed throat, thus ending the fight; the sweetest bite he had ever had, as he said later. From this gory incident came the warcry of the Cameron Clan, 'Sons of dogs, come and get flesh!'

Later, much to the relief of the redcoats, Locheil was persuaded by General Monk to make a truce with the English forces on honourable terms without being obliged to take the Oath.

Nine miles further on we come to Glenfinnan, at the head of Loch Shiel, one of the most historical and most photographed places in Scotland. Here stands the Prince Charles Edward Stuart monument, erected in 1815 by Alexander MacDonald of Glenaladale on the spot where the Royal Standard was raised on 19 August 1745 to mark the start of what was to be the Prince's tragic effort to recover 'a throne lost by the imprudence of his ancestors'. He had landed with only seven companions (The Seven Men of Moidart) at Loch nan Uamh (Loch of the Caves) over to the west, and sailed up Loch Shiel. Although the party was disappointed to find no supporters waiting at Glenfinnan, the Standard was raised by the Marquis of Tullibardine and the Prince declared King. It was not until several hours later that they were cheered by the arrival of the first of the army-to-be, a large force of Camerons under Locheil.

The figure at the top of the monument was set up there sixteen years after the monument was built, and there is some controversy as to whether it represents the Prince himself or a symbolic Highlander. Before leaving Glenfinnan have a look at the spectacular railway viaduct, 1248 feet in length and rising to 110 feet in the centre.

Over the watershed the road descends to Loch Eilt (Loch of the Hinds) which, with its islands on which Scots firs grow, embodies the essence of Highland scenery. This excellent fishing loch connects with the sea by the River Ailort, which flows in at the head of narrow, winding Loch Ailort opening on to the Sound of Arisaig. Loch Ailort is divided from Loch nan Uamh by the peninsula of Ardnish. All along the seaboard here there are magnificent views out to the western islands.

Prince Charlie landed from the French frigate *Du Teillay* on 5 August 1745 at the mouth of the Borrodale Burn, below Arisaig House, halfway along the north shore of Loch nan Uamh. Borrodale figures a number of times in the Prince's expedition. Much later, after his defeat at Culloden (a battle that should never have been fought, at least under the existing conditions), he slipped through a ring of strong naval and military forces and reached the Outer Isles, where he expected to be met and conveyed to safety in France by a French frigate. However, the ship could not penetrate the blockade in time to meet him, so with the help of Flora MacDonald, that heroic figure in Scottish history, he returned to the mainland at Mallaig, expecting to find the ship at Borrodale. Disappointed again, he was obliged in order to avoid capture to keep on the move, through mountain and glen, ragged and bearded but always cheerfully optimistic. It is perhaps not far from the truth that between April and September the Prince actually enjoyed his adventures, the fox with the English hunt always on his tail. His sheltered life had not yet undermined his stamina, and he must have had a magnetic personality to win the respect, care and loyalty of what was regarded as a nation of uncouth Highlanders. It is a lesson to everyone how those men spurned the offer of a reward of £30,000 for the betrayal of the man they regarded as their true King.

In Glenmoriston surrounded by the redcoats, he was impersonated by a Mackenzie officer who by sacrificing his life — and head, which was taken to Carlisle for identification — allowed his Prince the chance to escape. There is a cairn erected beside the road in Glenmoriston to the memory of this brave officer.

Returning again to Glenborrodale, the Prince found that at last the frigate was awaiting him, having evaded the English warships. He sailed away on 20 September 1746, never to return, on the frigate *L'Heureux* whose name must have been a sad echo of his false hopes.

Seven men figured twice in his wanderings; first, the seven original companions who landed with him, and the Seven Men of Moriston, a dedicated group of dispossessed farmers who swore to harass the redcoats by guerilla tactics — and did — and who sheltered the Prince for a short time in one of their hide-outs, the cave of Coireghoth (Corrie of the Winds) up Glen Doe at the head of Glenmoriston, on the eastern side of that well-known mountain group the Five Sisters of Kintail. We think too of the Seven Men of Knoydart — actually six — crofters who in 1948 were so exasperated by legal delays and obstructions to their claims for land in the Knoydart estates that they took over crofting lands and proceeded to cultivate them. Unfortunately, the Law speeded up at this point — probably under pressure from the laird — and the men were obliged to withdraw. These lands of Knoydart were cleared of people in 1853 — another example of the action of an absentee landlord, backed by the power of Privilege, replacing the father-figure of the old chiefs and ending an old way of life.

At Loch Cilltean, near Loch nan Uamh, the treasure of 30,000 Louis d'Or (mentioned earlier) was landed temporarily for safety and hidden in a wood, when the two French ships conveying the gold were being hard-pressed by a fleet of English frigates. It was then that the keg was broken open and a bag containing 700 coins stolen by the three defecting guards. They were never heard of again. Did they quarrel over the spoils and kill each other? Or does the stolen gold still lie there somewhere among the hills?

At Arisaig the road turns sharply north across the flat Mointeach Mhor to the bridge crossing the River Morar, one of the shortest rivers of its size, being only a mile long. Between the bridge and Loch Morar there are falls which have been harnessed to provide a small hydro-electric scheme. Loch Morar, almost 1100 feet deep, is another of these long, narrow fjord-like stretches of water running into the hills. It is the second deepest fresh water lake in Europe, exceeded in depth by a lake in Scandinavia. Roadless, only a track leads to its northern shore. Almost parallel to it is a similar loch, the sea loch of Nevis (no connection with Ben Nevis).

Between Arisaig and Morar there are bays of the famous 'Singing Sands', pure white sand which emits a faint 'creaking' or singing sound when trodden upon. This is a result of friction between individual grains of sand of uniform shape.

One stretch of road across a continuation of the flat ground beyond Morar station is called the Smooth Mile. Old folks will tell you this used to be haunted by the malevolent spectre of Colann gun Cheann, which not only terrified the people, but killed anyone appproaching it. This went on until a mighty member of the MacLeod clan from Raasay over in Skye, Mac-Gille Chaluinn by name, confronted the spectre in the early hours of the morning, choosing the hour when the powers of ghosts begin to wane with the approach of daylight. He overcame the headless spectre, but being a magnanimous man at heart, he responded to its plea to be allowed to carry on on condition that it reformed its habits and left the district.

In three or four miles we arrive at Mallaig, terminus of road and rail. The Mallaig railway from Fort William was opened in 1901 and is now under recurring threat of closure. Instead, it should be reorganised as a scenic attraction unrivalled in the British Isles and made both a well-advertised showpiece and an economic unit.

Mallaig lies in an excellent situation in a sheltered harbour looking out to the Sound of Sleat and the mountains of Skye. It is another starting-point for the islands, with regular Caledonian-MacBrayne sailings. Its small population of 1000 or so gives no indication of the town's importance as a fishing centre. In the early 1970s, when fishing conditions were stable, Mallaig was the most important herring fishing port in Europe, handling a third of the total catch in the British Isles. The town has a lobster storage pond and also a deep freeze and kippering facilities.

Mallaig is literally the end of the line, for between it and Kyle of Lochalsh, the road and rail terminus to the north, lies an area of twenty roadless miles, inaccessible mountains, glens and sea lochs, crossed only by tenuous tracks across the hills or along the shores; or preferably reached from the sea. The only road in the whole distance is a rough side road from Glenelg to Arnisdale, on the north shore of Loch Hourn, near which is the location described by Gavin Maxwell in his well-known book *Ring of Bright Water*, featuring the life of an otter. Glenelg itself is reached from the main road along Loch

Duich by the side road across Mam Rattachan which rises to 1100 feet in three miles.

The area south of Mallaig has one of the heaviest rainfalls in Britain, which incidentally accounts for the success of the rhododendrons and shrubs in such gardens as those of Arisaig House. In fact, along the whole north-west coast this rainfall, combined with a mild temperate summer and winter climate, allows sub-tropical shrubs, which have to be kept under glass in the famous Kew Gardens in London, to be grown freely in the open.

Before leaving Mallaig one should take a walk to the summit of Carn a'Gobhair (1794ft) a mile or two east of the township. From here there is a panoramic view, seldom equalled even in Scotland, of sea, lochs, mountains and islands, from the jagged Cuillin Mountains of Skye to the 'Cocktail Islands' of Rhum, Eigg, Muck and Canna, with the long peninsula of Ardnamurchan pointing out into the west.

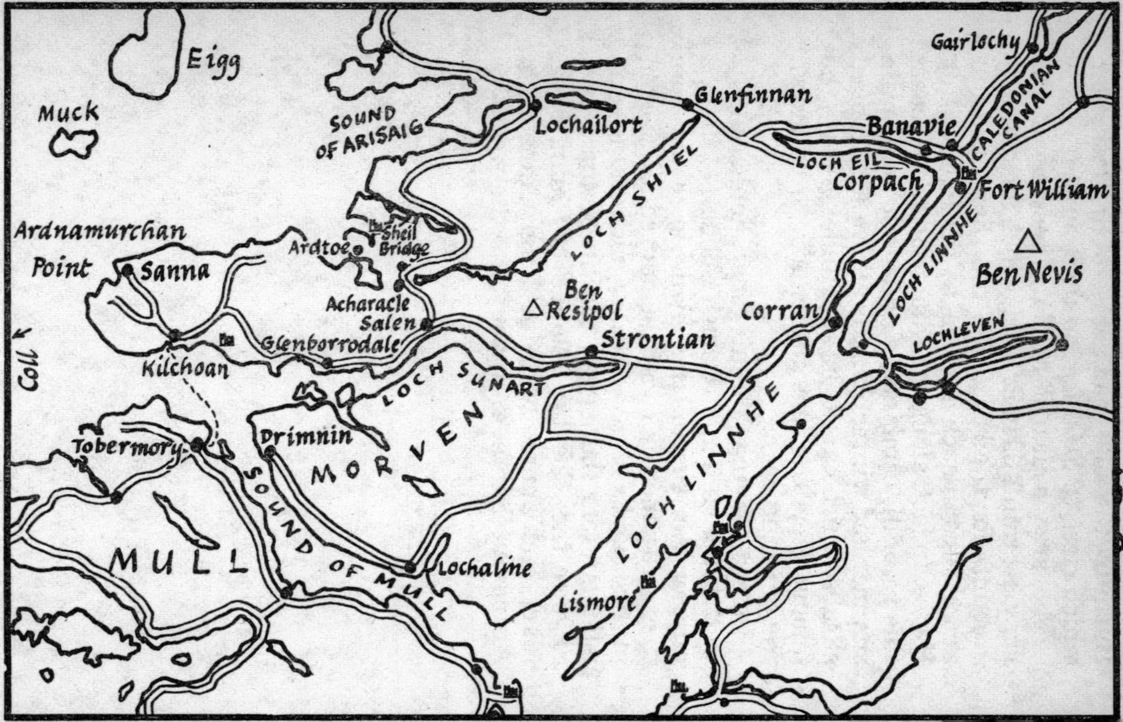
Eigg
Muck
SOUND OF ARISAIG
Lochailort
Glenfinnan
Gairlochy
CALEDONIAN CANAL
Banavie
LOCH EIL
Corpach
Fort William
Ben Nevis
LOCH SHIEL
Ardnamurchan Point
Sanna
Ardtoe
Sheil Bridge
Acharacle
Salen
Ben Resipol
Corran
LOCH LINNHE
LOCHLEVEN
Strontian
Glenborrodale
Kilchoan
Coll
LOCH SUNART
MORVEN
Drimnin
Tobermory
LOCH LINNHE
MULL
SOUND OF MULL
Lochaline
Lismore

Fort William to Ardnamurchan (58 miles) and Morvern (41 miles)

SOUTH OF THE MALLAIG ROAD LIES A rugged land of little roads and long miles, of lochs and grassy moorlands. Loch Sunart, narrow, sheltered and beautiful, almost cuts through the peninsula of Morvern, which is bounded on the south by the Sound of Mull. The district comprises Ardgour, Ardnamurchan, Moidart and Morvern, with Loch Linnhe to the east and the Sound of Arisaig to the west. The main approach from Fort William is by taking the main road to the south for nine miles to Corran Ferry and crossing to the Ardgour shore (five or six minutes) where the scattered communities of Ardgour and Clovulin lie along the sunny stretch of flat land backed by the high hills of Ardgour.

There is an alternative route for the leisured explorer, or for times when the ferry is suspended. This means taking the Mallaig road as far as Drumsallie, at the head of Loch Eil, then following the shore of the loch to its junction with Loch Linnhe, then along the shore by the winding secondary road 36 miles to Corran on the Ardgour side. An excellent new road runs from the ferry for 15 miles through Glen Tarbert to the village of Strontian near the head of Loch Sunart.

This township lies at the mouth of the Strontian River on land owned by the Government. It is a semi-industrialised community and has been since the early 18th century when lead mines were first opened up by Sir Alexander Murray of Stanhope. Other metals were also found, including Strontianite (called after the district), from which in 1808 Sir Humphrey Davy isolated the new element Strontium, well-known today through its association with atomic energy. Scotstown, one of the little centres in the glen, is where miners from the south were first housed.

Strontian is remembered, too, in another context, that of the Disruption that took place in 1843 in the Church of Scotland leading up to the formation of the Free Church. The reason for this was that the administration of the Church of Scotland was largely in the hands of the landowners and the privileged classes, much to the dissatisfaction of the people, especially in the North of Scotland. Here many parish ministers, who so often owed their livings to the patronage of the local lairds, were not guiltless of siding with them during the days of the Clearances and leaving their parishioners to their fate. Most of the people of Strontian seceded to the Free Church and sought a portion of land on which to build their own church. This the local landowner refused to grant, and put every obstacle in their way; but not to be outdone, the people acquired a boat suitable for the purpose and anchored it offshore as a place of worship. This was in 1846, and although it was blown ashore in a gale, it was still serviceable, and was used as a church until 1873, when at last land was obtained and a place of worship built.

Ben Resipol (2774ft) is the last of the higher hills before we proceed further west. It lies about four miles west of Strontian, and from its top another magnificent panorama can be seen. We follow the wooded shores of Loch Sunart to Salen, officially designated as Salen, Acharacle, to avoid confusion with Salen, Aros, in Mull. Here the road divides, one branch going northwards towards Acharacle and beyond, the other westwards into Ardnamurchan, and the little hamlet of Kilchoan that looks across the Sound of Mull to Ardmore, the northernmost tip of the island of Mull. There is a regular Caledonian-MacBrayne passenger ferry between Kilchoan and Tobermory in Mull, of great service to local people, for without it they would have to travel the 53 miles to Fort William for major requirements.

Like the centre of Mull, Ardnamurchan was a centre of violent volcanic action in the Tertiary Age. It is a rugged finger of land, the most westerly point in Great Britain; in fact, there is nearly half an hour's difference between the 'sun' time here and at Greenwich. The name means 'Headland of the Great Waves', and indeed it faces into the wild seas of the open Atlantic. Yachtsmen used to hoist a peat to the masthead as a proud announcement that they had safely rounded Ardnamurchan Point — we do not know if the practice is still followed these sophisticated days. Here there are many herds of red deer; the golden eagle also ranges far around and there are wild cats, foxes, otters and a great variety of birds. It is a paradise for the nature lover and also for the explorer of the byways. Little roads snake through the hills to tiny hamlets and unfrequented sandy beaches along the north shore of the peninsula, reaching as far as the tall lighthouse by what ends as a rough track passing through pleasant crofting land just short of the point. The lighthouse was designed by Alan Stevenson, uncle of Robert Louis Stevenson, and building began in 1849. Red granite from the Ross of Mull quarry was used in the final stages of completion.

This was once the land of the Clan MacIain, the progenitor of whom was Iain, a son of Angus Mor MacDonald of Islay. The Clan's great castle of Mingary, now in ruins, lies above the shore a mile short of Kilchoan, with its seagate facing on to the sea where the galleys used to come in. Since it was established in the 15th century, the building has had a chequered history. Visited in 1495 by James IV during a punitive expedition to the islands, it was unsuccessfully besieged by MacDonald of Lochalsh in 1515, but with more success in 1517, when it was taken and partly destroyed. In 1588 it was again besieged, this time by Maclean of Duart, with a contingent of Spanish soldiers from the Armada ship refitting in Tobermory Bay; but Maclean had to give up the siege under pressure from allies of MacIain's who rallied to his assistance. A relic of this event is the name of the bay in front of the castle — Port nan Spainndeach (Spaniard's Port or Bay). Finally, in the middle of the 17th century, Mingary came into the hands of the Campbells of Argyll.

MacIain, in his hey-day, was reputed to have been something of a pirate. Even in the 16th century there were still piratical raids in the Hebrides, chiefly by a few Danes and Norsemen.

The story told about MacIain describes how he painted one side of his boat black, the other white, and this, with changes in the colour of his sails, caused considerable confusion in trying to identify the raider, for it was hard to tell whether he was coming or going!

Before leaving Kilchoan, the explorer should take to the hills again and climb Ben Hiant, the Sacred or Fairy Hill, which rises from the shore three miles east of Kilchoan. Although only 1729 feet high, its isolation allows wonderful views of the whole area round about.

Returning now to Salen, on Loch Sunart, one can head north towards Acharacle and the Mallaig road. Acharacle and Shiel Bridge are passed by, scattered communities at the outflow end of Loch Shiel, where there is some of the finest salmon and seatrout fishing in Scotland, as there is also on the River Shiel that flows into Loch Moidart not far from Castle Tioram. A side road going left from Acharacle passes through little hamlets, notably Ardtoe, where, in an enclosed saltwater farm within a sheltered inlet, the White Fish Authority has been experimenting for some years with the rearing of sea fish, plaice in particular, from eggs.

Castle Tioram lies just beyond the end of another side road going north from Shiel Bridge. It lies halfway along the south shore of Loch Moidart and stands on a rocky eminence on Eilean Tioram (Dry Island) from which it takes its name. The term 'dry' means that it is an island which can be reached dryshod at low tide across a spit of sand. Built in the 14th century by the divorced wife of John MacDonald of Islay, the castle later became the seat of the MacDonalds of Clanranald and it is the subject of many tales of witchcraft and battle. With its own well of fresh water in the floor of the kitchen it could hold out for a lengthy time against a siege. It was captured only once, and then by a trick. The Campbells had been besieging the place unsuccessfully for weeks. Pretending to give up, they sailed away in their galleys, and on seeing this the defending MacDonalds began to disperse to their homes. However, the Campbells turned back, attacked the castle and overwhelmed the few guards left behind; but on learning how they had been tricked, the infuriated MacDonalds returned in such force that the Campbells were driven out.

The castle is now in ruins. It is said to have been deliberately set on fire on the orders of Allan Mor of Moidart, for when setting out to join up with the 1715 Jacobite uprising he had a presentiment that he would never return. Once he was out of sight, he ordered the place to be put to the torch.

Loch Shiel is long and narrow and in a picturesque setting between the mountains stretching for fourteen miles to Glenfinnan. As on a number of other long Highland lochs, in days gone by a small steamer used to serve the public. Near the west end there is the sacred island of Saint Finnan where there are the remains of the Saint's chapel. It was a burial island, one half of which was reserved for Protestants, the other for Roman Catholics. Most of the great chiefs of Clanranald were interred here.

Until recent years the road ended at the head of Loch Moidart, but in the 1970s it was extended by building a new connecting road, following old tracks through Glenuig to the mouth of Lochailort, continuing along the shore of the loch to meet the Fort William-Mallaig road at Lochailort village and railway station.

But we now return to Strontian and the head of Loch Sunart to explore the last of the little roads of the mainland of Argyll. Here the road to Morvern and the Sound of Mull strikes to the south above high water mark at the head of the loch and continues for four miles along the lovely, well-wooded shoreline. It then turns inland up Glen Liddesdale, a long steady pull of two miles to the watershed at 800 feet, with fine views looking back towards Ben Resipol and the Ardgour mountains. We are now in Morvern, a name meaning 'Sea Gap' descriptive of the stretch of level land along Glen Tarbert dividing Loch Linnhe from Loch Sunart.

It is rather a bleak run across the grassy moorlands and rounded hills of Morvern, but by an excellent road. 19 miles from Strontian and 32 from Corran Ferry, we come to Lochaline, on the Sound of Mull. The name *Aline* means 'beautiful' in Gaelic, which well describes both this sheltered loch and the approach along the last four miles of wooded glen beside the River Aline. At the head of Loch Aline we pass the little hamlet of Larachbeg, one of the centres to which the inhabitants of the lonely islands of St Kilda were evacuated in 1930 when life in this remote island group became no longer viable. Here they soon settled down in the new environment. Kinlochaline Castle — or Tower House — stands above and to the west of the point where the River Aline flows into the loch. Built during the 15th century by the Macleans of Duart, it was extensively damaged in the 16th century during the recurring disputes between the Macleans and the Campbells and has been in ruins ever since, although some efforts have been made to restore some of the stonework and make the interior weatherproof.

The village of Lochaline has a substantial pier with a slipway beside it which is used by the ferry across to Mull. This is a six-car ferryboat that shuttles to and fro during the day — fewer runs in the off-season — doing the 15-minute run to the slipway at Fishnish on the Mull side of the Sound. Apprehensive drivers may find it rather primitive, because while they drive on normally on the one side of the crossing, they have to reverse up the slipway on the other. However, the crews are careful and extremely helpful and the increasing use of this route to Mull may see the service up-graded in the future.

Along the western shore of Loch Aline, lying under the surface, there are deposits of silica sand, 99% pure, a valuable product for the manufacture of high-grade optical and precision glass. It was first exploited in 1940 when it was almost impossible to obtain imports of this commodity, and since then probably up to two million tons have been extracted, crushed, and loaded by conveyor belt into coasters at the pier. The pier is also a calling-point for the occasional extra run by the Oban to Craignure car ferry. Also on the shores of Loch Aline are outcrops of fossiliferous limestone, where interesting specimens can be picked up.

On the eastern side of the entrance to the loch, on the flat promontory, are the substantial ruins of 14th-century Ardtornish Castle, principal seat of the Lords of the Isles at the height of their power. In 1466 a treaty was negotiated here between the Lords of the Isles and Edward IV of England to overthrow the kings of Scotland, for the Lords of the Isles held that the Celtic line of descent was the correct one, not the indirect Norman line which had earlier been substituted, and the Lords of the Isles had been one of the claimants. Ardtornish is mentioned by Sir Walter Scott in his *Lord of the Isles*.

A high escarpment in which many descending streams have cut deep chimneys runs east for about a mile beyond Ardtornish Castle. In strong south-west gales after heavy rain these are checked in their descent and blown back like smoke over the edge above. Perhaps this is why locally the cliff used to be called 'The Stills'. This is a spectacular phenomenon common to all the high west-facing cliffs during stormy weather. When Ardtornish was a stronghold of the MacDonalds, captives who met with the displeasure of the Castle Lord were hauled to the top of the cliff and hurled over to their deaths on the rocks below.

One of the two medieval Parish Churches in Morvern was at Lochaline and in the churchyard of Keil Church there are traces of one of them. Here, too, are old grave slabs marking the last resting-places of local chiefs and men of importance. A Spanish Princess is supposed to have been buried here or hereabouts after her body was found on the shore nearby; perhaps the same Princess as was reputed to have been on the Armada galleon blown up in Tobermory Bay.

From Lochaline a secondary road continues along the Sound of Mull to Drimnin. This was the home of three generations of famous Gaelic ministers, of whom Dr Norman MacLeod was the best known. Fuinary, close by, was the title adopted by the Rev George MacLeod (Lord MacLeod of Fuinary) when he was honoured for his dedicated work in the founding and continuation of the Iona Community since 1938. The haunting Gaelic song *Farewell to Fuinary* was composed by his father when he moved to Campbeltown.

An alternative road to Lochaline from Corran Ferry runs from Inversanda Bay on Loch Linnhe, just south of the ferry, and joins the main road not far from the summit of Liddesdale, but the main road is preferable.

So we leave you at this point on the slipway at Lochaline Pier, ready to cross over to Mull and continue our exploring there. However, this is the back door to Mull, so to speak. The main crossing is from Oban by the luxury 50-car ferry run by Caledonian-MacBrayne between the modern roll-on roll-off pier facilities beside the railway pier and Craignure pier in Mull. The rest of this book will take you through Mull and its adjacent islands — not forgetting the sacred island of Iona and of course Staffa — and tell you about its people, traditions and folklore.

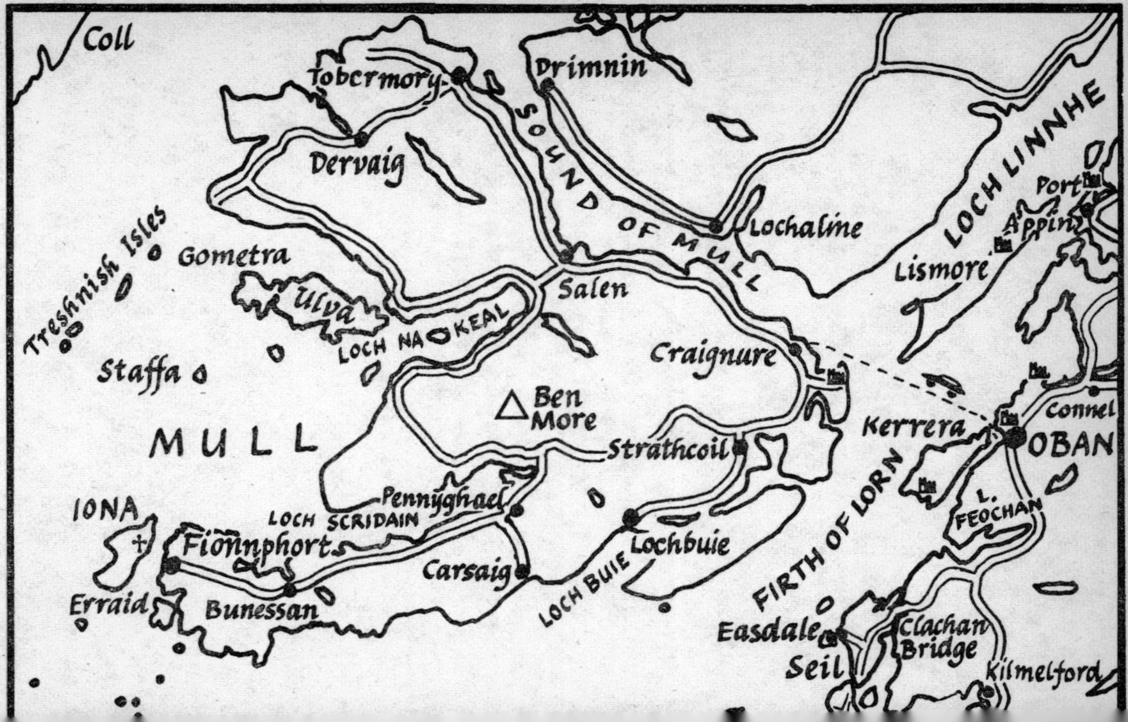
Coll
Tobermory
Drimnin
Dervaig
SOUND OF MULL
Lochaline
LOCH LINNHE
Port Appin
Lismore
Treshnish Isles
Gometra
Ulva
Salen
LOCH NA KEAL
Craignure
Staffa
Ben More
MULL
Strathcoil
Kerrera
Connel
OBAN
Pennyghael
LOCH SCRIDAIN
IONA
Fionnphort
L. FEOCHAN
FIRTH OF LORN
Lochbuie
LOCH BUIE
Carsaig
Erraid
Bunessan
Easdale
Clachan Bridge
Seil
Kilmelford

The Isle of Mull

Introduction

WE HAVE LEFT YOU ON THE PIER AT Oban, probably watching the activities around the fishing boats tied up alongside as you wait for the Mull ferry to round the point of Kerrera opposite Dunollie Castle. There used to be ranks of fisher girls here on the pier cheerfully gutting seemingly endless baskets of herring: but no longer in these days of herring shortage, and when our coastal fisheries no longer seem to be our own. Or perhaps you were relaxing beside the slipway at Lochaline enjoying the peace and quiet. In either case you are looking across to the hills of Mull that beckon you over to new explorations.

Now, why choose Mull from all these fascinating islands of the Hebrides? The answer is simple: Mull is both unique and accessible. It has all the attributes of a Hebridean island, yet has close affinities with the mainland. It just fails to be a southern extension of Morvern by the dividing arm of the Sound of Mull which is only two miles wide at its narrowest. Mull has been called a microcosm of all pertaining to both the Highlands and Islands.

Plant life is influenced by the proximity of the mainland, yet it is truly Hebridean, with some specimens peculiar to the island. Bird life is interesting too; for instance, the ptarmigan, game bird of the high Highland hills, often frequents the hills above Craignure. Mull is probably the most intensely-researched geological area in the world, centring on the ancient volcanic district of mid-Mull. It is an island of scenic contrasts, from the flat crofting lands and sandy beaches of the Ross of Mull, through the high mountains, to the moorlands and even 'steps and stairs' of ancient eroded lava flows of the northern district. The coastline ends in great stretches of cliffs to the south, west and north, in one part up to 1000 feet high, and in the dark rocks of the north there is the occasional little beach of dazzling white sand. The Sound of Mull is less interesting with its flat rocky shoreline.

Such natural features are of course found in other islands such as Skye or Islay, but in addition Mull has such unique curiosities as a Fossil Tree which is one of the wonders of Europe, as well as the fantastic basaltic columns of Staffa and certain lesser-known but almost as attractive stretches of the coastline.

Mull has social factors all of its own. For instance, the world's smallest professional theatre lies near the village of Dervaig in the north, where, too, there is a combination of museum and tableaux presenting housing conditions and artifacts of the local people up to 200 years ago, which has received two national awards. There is a resident School of Painting in one of the island's most picturesque settings.

Mull has been selected as a background for certain scenes in three major movies, *Where Eight Bells Toll*, *Madam Sin*, and *The Eye of the Needle*. Between Craignure Pier and Torosay Castle a narrow gauge railway, which will be the only one of its kind in the Hebrides, is approaching completion as a tourist attraction. One of Britain's important car rallies, The Tour of Mull Rally, has been run on the island every year since the 1960s by the Mullard Blackburn 2300 Club over main roads and forestry tracks, and attracting up to 130 leading British drivers.

In spring, there is a Musical Festival, the Festival of Mull, which lasts for a week. In between are the usual ceilidh-concerts, Agricultural Shows, Highland Games, Clay Pigeon Shoots, Sheep Dog Trials — and all the rest. Tobermory has even its own distillery that produces a very acceptable blend and a malt whisky calculated to revive the most flagging of spirits — if you will excuse the pun. Add to all that the story of the Spanish Armada galleon containing a treasure of golden ducats, which was blown up in 1588 and whose timbers lie deep in the silt at the bottom of Tobermory Bay.

There are angling facilities for salmon, sea-trout, brown and rainbow trout. The trout fishing is particularly rewarding on the lochs, for the rivers are small and depend on flood waters for successful salmon fishing. Sea anglers are well catered for and will find fishing both attractive and varied. There is golf, hill walking, pony trekking, bird watching and local cruising and, for the erudite, geology, botany, archaeology — a variety of interests that make summer days too short.

But greatest of all lying off the south-west corner of Mull there is the island of Iona whose atmosphere takes us back 1400 years. This atmosphere is summarised by the writer of this book in his earlier work *The Isle of Mull* in the words:

> Iona, the island of St Columba, called in the past the University of the north, is steeped in history and tradition. Here we can see the moon on royal tombstones gleam and read in carved coats of arms the story of men who lived, preached, fought and died, back to the dawn of Christianity in this part of the world. The atmosphere is well conveyed by Dr Johnson's words: "We are now treading that illustrious Island, which was once the luminary of the Caledonian regions, whence savage clans and roving barbarians derived the benefits of knowledge and the blessings of religion . . . That man is little to be envied whose . . . piety would not grow warmer among the ruins of Iona."

In Mull the motorist will find a surprising mileage of roads — up to 150 — although most of them are narrow, with passing-places, blind corners and sharp gradients, and unfenced, so do beware of sheep. The walker, whether on hill or path, will find a wide and interesting choice of byways, with no prohibition on access except, of course, in the case of purely private policies. The hills of Mull are more kindly than the austere peaks of the mainland and their ascent is more of a stiff walk. However, one unenviable problem is shared by Mull with the whole West of Scotland — the Highland midge, whose attentions during windless weather in summer and autumn can be acute. A supply of anti-midge cream is a wise extra.

Behind all this we have a store of history, folklore and traditions, of song and music, for which Mull has always been famous; and as we begin our leisurely exploration of the island we shall try to convey something of this rich heritage.

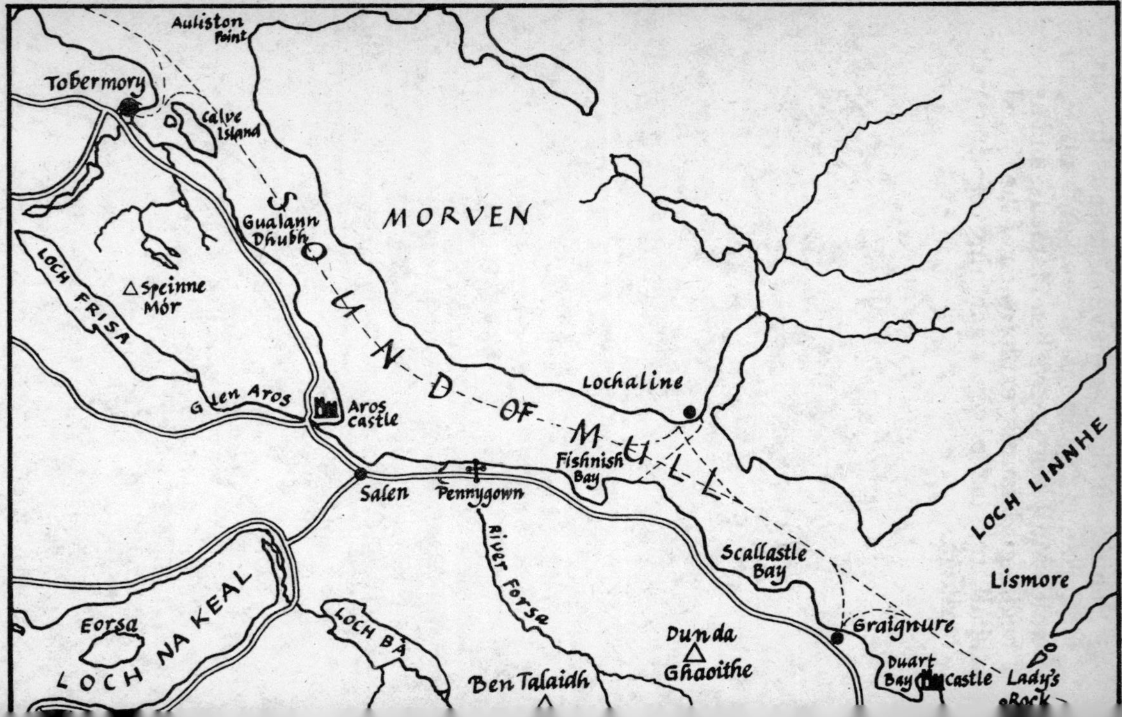
Auliston Point
Tobermory
Calve Island
MORVEN
Gualann Dhubh
SOUND OF MULL
LOCH FRISA
Speinne Mór
Glen Aros
Aros Castle
Lochaline
Fishnish Bay
Salen
Pennygown
River Forsa
Scallastle Bay
LOCH LINNHE
Lismore
LOCH NA KEAL
Eorsa
LOCH BÀ
Ben Talaidh
Dun da Ghaoithe
Craignure
Duart Bay
Castle
Lady's Rock

Craignure to Tobermory (24 miles)

THE MAIN CROSSING, WHICH TAKES about 40 minutes, is by the Caledonian-MacBrayne 50-car ferry, which in the summerseason makes five return trips daily to Craignure. The modern roll-on roll-off facilities have transformed the handling of traffic, and Mull roads are busy during the season. Formerly a small mailboat used to zig-zag its way on one return trip daily from Tobermory to Oban, taking 3½ hours each way, calling at four intermediate points along the Sound of Mull, Drimnin, Salen, Lochaline and Craignure. How we used to pity the poor passengers who were conveyed in all weathers in an open boat from the shore to the ship's side at Drimnin and Craignure. However, the building of the Craignure pier in 1964 moved the centre of communications from Tobermory to Craignure, with its much shorter crossing distance to Oban, and the 24 miles to Tobermory are now completed by MacBrayne's motor coaches. This form of transport also connects the ferry with the Ross of Mull and Iona.

It is sometimes thought that MacBrayne's ships have gone to the other extreme with their luxury lounges, bars, observation lounges, and so on, with an eye on the tourist trade rather than providing a less costly vessel that would cater for the basic needs of the island communities. However, Caledonian-MacBrayne is under the direction of the Secretary of State and decisions are approved at that level. Fares and freight charges are a crippling burden on island economy.

We cross the open Firth of Lorne on the way to Mull. Opening to the south-west and the Atlantic, it can be stormy in the winter time, but normally it is a delightful sail, with views of the mainland hills from Ben Nevis and the Glencoe peaks, by Cruachan, down to the distant islands of Scarba and the Garvellochs. Halfway across we pass between Lismore lighthouse, at the southern tip of that island, and the Lady Rock, a tidal reef carrying a warning beacon. There is a miniature tide-rip here where the tidal flows of the Sound of Mull and Loch Linnhe meet.

The Lady Rock has been so-called since the early 16th century, when the Macleans of Duart were the most powerful clan in the area. One particular chief, Lachlan Cattanach, was 'one of the few bad chiefs of the Clan Maclean' — for you may recall Neil Munro's quotation in one of his books, 'The Macleans were the gentlemanly fellows, but the MacDonalds were the warriors'. This chief was married to Elizabeth, daughter of the second Earl of Argyll, but it is said, she failed to present him with an heir, so he sought to get rid of her. This he did by having her marooned and tied down on this tidal reef off Lismore, expecting that the next high tide would solve his problem. However, her frantic cries were heard by passing fishermen, who rescued her and landed her over on the Lorne shore, from where she arrived back at her father's castle at Inveraray.

Shortly afterwards Duart, on a visit to Inveraray, hypocritically bemoaned the death of his wife, only to be confronted by her in person, much to his confusion. Her brother, the new Earl, took no steps to avenge the deed, but a year or two later Duart was killed in Edinburgh by another brother, Campbell of Achallader. This tragic tale is used as a plot in the poem *Glenara* by Thomas Campbell, who later became Poet Laureate. As a young man he tutored for a year or two a family at Sunipol, near Calgary in the north of Mull, and his poetic imagination was fired by the folklore of Mull. *Lord Ullin's Daughter*, another poem, was a further inspiration, and some of his greater works reveal the influence of his stay.

Landing at Craignure you are faced at the pierhead with a decision: whether to go right for north and central Mull, or south for the Ross and Iona. We suggest you take the northern circuit first, reserving Iona, Glen More and Duart until later. The road from Craignure to Salen, and its continuation to the south, has been modernised out of all recognition. Until the 1970s it was like some of the present side roads and quite inadequate for the increasing traffic, especially the coaches. We repeat the warning on livestock on the unfenced roads, where sheep and lambs can be concealed in scrub and bracken and emerge suddenly in front of the car. High above the road to the left you see the long high ridge of Dun da Ghaoithe (2512ft), a tongue-twister meaning the stronghold of the two winds, so called because the configuration at the top deflects the wind in all directions.

A mile from Craignure, past the new Isle of Mull Hotel, you will see the little golf-course opened here in 1979. There was a rough course here back in the 1920s, when golf enthusiasm hit Mull and about six courses were in use, some of only six holes. Only Tobermory and Iona survived — they had been in existence long before the 20s. For much of the 14 miles to Salen the road follows the shore, along the old raised beach with old shallow sea caves along the landward side. We pass the junction of the new mile-long road through the plantations to the slipway at Fishnish Bay, which looks across to Lochaline. A few miles later we see the walls of ruined Pennygown Chapel rising above the old cemetery to the right of the road. Measuring 39¾ by 17 feet, this is one of the fourteen medieval chapels scattered through Mull. A loop of the old road passes the unusual access to the enclosure, consisting of steps rising to the top of the wall and descending on the other side, designed to exclude livestock without breaking the wall to erect a gate.

Inside the chapel note the ornamental shaft of an old cross, and outside, the two recumbent grave slabs, one with the carved effigy of a warrior, the other the elaborate Celtic design indicating a woman. These are said to cover the bodies of that same Lachlan Cattanach and his wife — presumably a more acceptable one — who were refused interment within the holy ground of the chapel itself, but who were buried as near to its walls as possible. This was because they were accused of dabbling in witchcraft, for instance, the roasting of live cats whose squalling conjured up the Evil One himself to do their bidding. Nearby there is a fairy knoll whose inhabitants wove a spell which destroyed the roof of the chapel as fast as it was built — a typical tale from the past almost duplicated in the building of the Cathedral in Iona, when even Columba himself was obliged to bury alive one of his disciples, St Oran, to placate the indigenous evil spirits of Iona. A day or two later, when Columba in a fit of curiosity, ordered Oran's face to be uncovered, he hastily ordered the earth to be flung in again when the interred disciple began to describe how the nether regions were not half as bad as they were described to the people!

Just beyond here the River Forsa is passed, a good little salmon river flowing into the sea not far from Mull's airstrip that lies beside the Log Hotel. The landing strip, grass over gravel, 3000 feet by 90 feet, was built in 1966 by the Engineers' Regiment. Loganair used to run regular flights from Glasgow, but now it is used by the occasional private flight. Glen Forsa is a wide fertile glen running inland to the symmetrical bulk of Ben Talaidh (2496ft), about which more later.

Two miles further on the new road ends at the village of Salen standing at the eastern corner of its bay. Designed and built in 1808 by Lt General Lachlan MacQuarie, 'Father of Australia', within whose estate it then lay, it is now a busy little place, a centre of the road system, connecting across the three-miles isthmus with Loch na Keal and the western coast road. Its postal address is Salen, Aros, after the name of the local district. The word *Aros* is Scandinavian, meaning an inlet or estuary, as in *Aarhus*, Denmark. Around the coast of Mull one place name in four is of Scandinavian origin, a legacy handed down from Viking days. At Salen we leave the central mountainous district and cross into the quieter north, where no hill exceeds 1456 feet, and where the level lava flows have been eroded and cut back into excellent examples of 'steps and stairs' or 'Trap' scenery (Scandinavian, *trappa*, a step), marking the harder and softer rocks of successive flows.

The road follows the shoreline to the head of the estuary to the road junction, the main road going right for Tobermory across the bridge spanning the Aros River (a good little salmon river, but private), the other continuing along the riverside up Glenaros, then crossing over to Glen Bellart and the village of Dervaig 12 miles away. Just before you reach the bridge on the left-hand side you will notice a small field backed by trees, which is the ground used annually to hold the Mull and Morvern Agricultural Show established in 1832.

There is a little-known story told about this field — Dal na Sassunach, or Field of the Englishman, it is called. In 1609 a fleet under Lord Ochiltree was sent from Ayr to discipline the unruly west-coast chiefs and anchored here below old Aros Castle. The unsuspecting chiefs were invited on board ostensibly to listen to a sermon by the Bishop of the Isles, actually to find themselves confined on board and on their way to the south, from which they were allowed to return only after giving assurances of their good behaviour. When the fleet raised anchor and sailed away an English soldier failed to return in time and was left behind.

He was an adaptable man who resigned himself to a new life, taking service as a shepherd with McArthur, that gifted maestro, trained under the great MacCrimmon of Skye, who had set up his own college of piping on or near the island of Ulva. Strange to say, the Englishman found himself to be a natural piper, with the gift of memorising a new tune at one hearing, and able to copy exactly the fingering on the chanter. When tending the sheep he used to practise on a borrowed chanter or even on lengths of stick.

As McArthur used to walk along he was continually practising intricate fingering on the walking stick he held behind his back, and as the Englishman walked behind with other servants he faithfully memorised every movement. There came a day when McArthur had invited a number of critical friends to hear his interpretation of a very intricate pipe tune — *The Battle of the Birds* — of which the original air is now lost. By an unfortunate coincidence the English shepherd, innocently thinking to give his employer a pleasant surprise, came out in front of the gathering playing on a borrowed set of bagpipes an exact rendering of this tune which he had picked up when watching McArthur.

The great piper was mortified and incensed by this insult, however unintended. He and his sons drew their dirks and attacked the bewildered amateur piper, who fled towards the only sanctuary he could think of — the place where he had landed. Here, in the field beside the bridge, he was overtaken by the McArthurs and put to death.

The ruins of old Aros Castle lie about half a mile beyond the bridge and are reached by a farm road to the right above the cutting. This is a massive 13th-century castle built originally by the MacDougalls of Lorne, then taken over by the Lords of the Isles, becoming a stronghold second only in importance to Ardtornish, across the Sound of Mull at Lochaline. A mile or so further on a forestry road branches to the left. through the plantations to Loch Frisa, Mull's longest loch (four miles) with an indigenous stock of fighting, red-fleshed trout and the chance of a salmon or seatrout. Boats to fish may be hired from Salen Post Office or from the Forestry Commission office.

Four miles from Tobermory the road rises above the Sound of Mull at the Ghulann Dubh, or Black Steep, with splendid views back to Oban or north towards Ardnamurchan. It then descends through woodlands, with scattered houses beginning to appear, to the crossroads at Tom a'Mhuillin Bridge which crosses the Tobermory River, where there is a choice of roads to the Main Street and waterfront, to the Upper Village, or inland to the west. Keeping the river to our left, with its cataracts and a picturesque waterfall, we descend by a steep hill to the final bend, beyond which lies the colourful Main Street and the wide-tree-fringed spread of Tobermory Bay, the finest bay in the Hebrides.

Tobermory

TOBERMORY, *TOBAR MHOIRE*, WHICH means 'Well of Mary', is the capital of Mull. Until 1975 when the area was absorbed into the unwieldy Region of Strathclyde, it was an independent Burgh, perhaps the smallest in Scotland with a population of only 600 or so, although 100 years ago when it was raised to Burgh status, it had about 2000 inhabitants. It is a well-wooded, south-facing sun-trap on the north shore of this safe and sheltered anchorage, backed by steep slopes up which roads lead to the Upper Village. There are three piers, MacBrayne's, the Old Pier (now owned by the local Fishing Association) and a rough jetty in front of the distillery where the Tobermory River enters the sea. In a corner of the shingly shore beside the Old Pier a sandy strip has been created by bringing in loads of sand and dumping them there, much to the delight of the children in the summertime.

Like Ullapool and other West Coast ports, Tobermory was established as a fishing base in 1789 by the British Fisheries Society; but fish, especially herring, became scarce, and Oban, thirty miles nearer the south and on the mainland — and especially when the railway was extended to there — became far more convenient. Although the town failed to become an important fishing centre, its original design remains in its Old Pier, some of the Main Street buildings, the lay-out of the Upper Village, and certain grazing and peat-cutting rights on the moorlands above the town. Of course from early times there must have been a small settlement here near the chapel of St Mary, the ruins of which are in the old cemetery to the left of the entrance gate. The cemetery also contains several old grave slabs, almost certainly of the Clan MacKinnon, whose lands these were until the Clan was driven away by the Macleans. The exact site of the original well is not known, but it must have been in the hollow lying below the commemoration fountain near the cemetery.

Tobermory is probably best known for its associations with a Spanish galleon sunk in the hard deep silt under ten fathoms of water about 400 yards off MacBrayne's Pier. This was identified as the *Florencia*, one of the storm-tossed galleons of the Spanish Armada escaping round the north of Scotland, which called in here for stores and re-fitting in 1588. Scotland as an independent country was not involved in the war with Spain. Maclean of Duart made a bargain with Don Ferreira, Captain of the *Florencia*, whereby in return for the services of 100 Spanish soldiers, Duart would provide the required assistance. Duart used those auxiliaries for an attack on Mingary Castle, over in Ardnamurchan, which failed, as we have already described.

Seeing the great ship almost ready to sail, Duart sent his kinsman, Donald Glas of Morvern, to collect the payments said to have been owing by the Spanish, but not only did the Captain refuse to pay, but he would not allow Donald Glas to leave the ship. In despair at the failure of his mission, and hearing the preparations for setting sail, Donald Glas managed to lay a powder train to the magazine which he touched off, blowing up the ship and himself with it. The explosion was violent and it is said that one of the cooks was hurled across the water into a cleft in the low cliff above the Main Street — other details of the explosion have been handed down. For many years a portion of the stern castle showed above the water.

Of course, there is another version of the destruction of the galleon. Seemingly there was a Spanish princess on board, a bewitching lady with whom Duart fell head over heels in love, to the neglect of his own lady sitting grimly waiting in Duart Castle. She invoked the services of the greatest witches of her time to end the romance and arrange for the safe return of Duart to her wrathful presence. The Doiteag Muileach, the Witch of Mull, was one of them, but she mixed up her spells and sank a passing galley of the MacDonalds, which led to some awkward inter-clan explanations later. Nor were any of the other local practitioners more successful, until the Maclean lady finally turned to the Gormshuil Mor, the great blue-eyed witch of Lochaber. Assuming the shape of a cormorant, this witch flew over to a strategic spot between the standing stones at Baliscate, above the Bay, and there she called up an army of huge brindled fairy cats, which swam out to the ship, stormed the bulwarks and put every member of the crew to the claw. One terrified sailor dashed down into the magazine, followed by one bristling cat, but the sparks from its fur set off the powder, and up went ship, cats, sailors and princess, the lot!

Now, this galleon is reputed to have carried a treasure of 30 million golden ducats intended for the pay of the Duke of Parma's army when it had landed in England. This was said to be stored below the gun deck, which must also have been near the magazine. Other accounts dispute that the galleon was the *Florencia*, suggesting other names, and questioning the presence of a treasure. We cannot trace any exact documentation to support the popular theory. In spite of many salvage operations conducted since the 17th century, including expeditions during the present century using the most modern equipment, little but items normally carried on shipboard were ever found. One fine Cellini cannon was raised and stands in front of Inveraray Castle; the Duke of Argyll was granted the rights of recovery over all Spanish ships sunk round the coasts of Mull. So where is the treasure? Scattered over the seabed by the explosion? Retrieved and hidden before the wreck vanished? Tradition says the ducats lie buried under old Aros Castle — but was the treasure ever there . . .?

Tobermory is connected with another great story of the sea, which seems sadly to have been forgotten, even although it belongs to a period as recent as 1939-45. You can read the whole story in Richard Baker's book *The Terror of Tobermory*. The town became a training centre for an anti-submarine establishment in the War of the Atlantic and the administration centre was the Western Isles Hotel that stands above

MacBrayne's Pier. Here, under the unorthodox and exacting régime introduced by Vice Admiral Sir Gilbert Stephenson ('The Terror'), newly-commissioned anti-submarine escort vessels up to destroyer size were brought up to a state of such efficiency in two weeks of intensive training — a fraction of the usual time required — that the Tobermory base accounted for no less than 130 enemy U-boats and 40 aircraft. Over 1000 ships and a quarter of a million men passed through the centre during the war and Tobermory was described as the most disciplined and efficient base in the British Isles. No wonder it was referred to as 'The Cradle of Victory in the Atlantic'.

However, the strategic value of Tobermory Bay was soon forgotten. The structure of MacBrayne's Pier has deteriorated so much due to lack of maintenance since the War that it is threatened with closure. It is estimated that it would cost £300,000 to repair, but no-one will accept responsibility. In view of its economic and strategic value in the north of Mull it would be reprehensible on the part of the authorities to let it die.

Tobermory is a busy place in the summer with three main hotels, many boarding houses and private accommodation, a Youth Hostel and a useful Information Centre in Main Street. In the town you will find a wide selection of the special interests already described for Mull as a whole. The little golf-course is run by the Western Isles Hotel and the views along the Sound of Mull from the course must be full compensation for many a wayward shot.

The Tobermory Angling Club caters for trout fishers in the three Mishnish Lochs within four miles, where brown trout of two to three pounds are to be caught. In the Aros Lake, across the Bay, rainbow trout up to 14½ pounds have been caught. Loch Torr, five miles distant, has sea-trout (with the odd chance of a salmon), brown and rainbow trout. It is regularly stocked with rainbows up to five pounds, and permits to fish can be obtained in the Tackle Shop, Main Street.

Tobermory is a good centre for walking. A path runs from the pier along the shore under the wooded slopes to the lighthouse of Rudha nan Gall, where the high cliffs of Bloody Bay rise just around the corner. In this bay in 1480 Angus Og defeated his father John, Lord of the Isles, who was allied with Maclean of Duart, in one of the most sanguinary sea fights in the Hebrides, when the sea was red with blood — hence the name of the bay. The return walk can be along the tops of the cliffs. Another favourite walk is by the path skirting the bay from the distillery, reaching Aros Park at the south side of the Bay where the lake stands among beds of rhododendrons surrounded by a ring of cliffs. The mansion house of Aros used to stand here, but when the Forestry Commission took over the policies they demolished the house, set up a car park, and presented the area to the township as a public park. The park can also be reached the easy way by car entering from the lodge gates two miles back along the Salen road.

Tobermory is a musical place, centre for the Mull Festival Week, with ceilidh-concerts and informal musical nights in the various hotels. One of these is the Mishnish Hotel, run by Bobby MacLeod, the well-known accordionist, whose repertoire owes much to his inherited knowledge of pipe tunes and old Gaelic airs. Here you will listen to the traditional music of the sea and the Hebridean islands; not what some people uncharitably describe as 'Haggis Music', but tunes with the tug of the oars, the lap of the waves, the roar of the breakers in them. There is one sad tune *Caol Muile* (The Sound of Mull) based on one of the ancient chants of the monks of Iona.

Much more could be written about the town, but the Information Centre will be glad to supply you with full details.

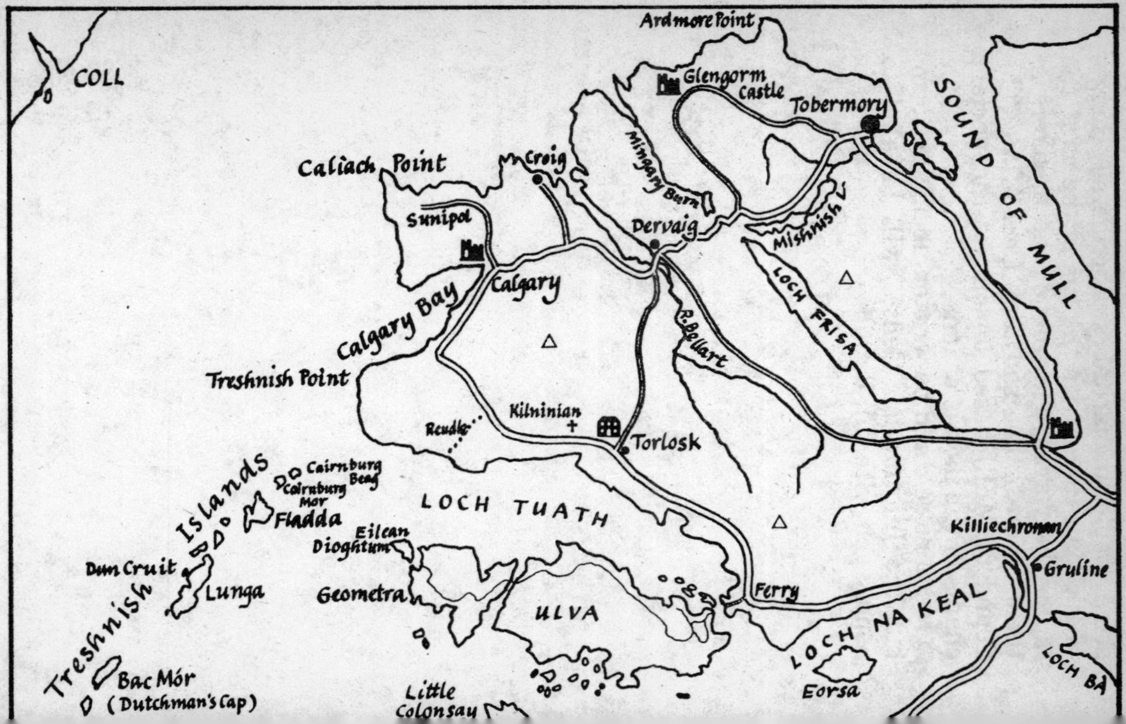
COLL
Ardmore Point
Glengorm Castle
Tobermory
SOUND OF MULL
Caliach Point
Croig
Mingary Burn
Mishnish
Sunipol
Dervaig
Calgary
LOCH FRISA
Calgary Bay
R. Bellart
Treshnish Point
Kilninian
Reudle
Torlosk
Cairnburg Beag
Cairnburg Mor
Fladda
LOCH TUATH
Treshnish Islands
Eilean Dioghtum
Killiechronan
Dun Cruit
Lunga
Geometra
ULVA
Ferry
Gruline
LOCH NA KEAL
Bac Mór
(Dutchman's Cap)
Little Colonsay
Eorsa
LOCH BA

North Mull: From Tobermory by Dervaig, Calgary and Torloisk to Gruline (31 miles)

CONTINUING ON OUR RATHER LEISURELY exploration, we take the Dervaig road above the township, one of the most tortuous yet fascinating roads in Mull. Less than a mile from the start there is a side road leading to Glengorm across bare moorlands and through forestry plantations, with tracks leading down to ruined deserted villages lying above the cliffs and rocky shores. Glengorm Castle — a fine Victorian mansion house — stands high above the coast with uninterrupted views north to Ardnamurchan and the islands. The scattered community here used to be called Sorne. The name was changed when a new laird took over and built this new mansion house, incidentally evicting tenants from three or four holdings to make sufficient suitable land available. Seeking a name for the house he asked an old local woman for her advice. She suggested he should call the place Glengorm — the Blue Glen. Delighted with the name, he adopted it, little knowing that the cynical old woman was commemorating for all time the occasions when the glen was indeed blue with the smoke of burning cot houses; for this was an area of evictions and Clearances. In fact, the north-west of Mull was one of the worst-affected areas, callously cleared of its people to make way for sheep, and when that industry was worked out, for sporting estates. The evidence given at the belated Commission of Enquiry in the 1890s makes bitter reading.

Tracks lead from Glengorm to Dervaig and round the coastline. The old Castle of Dunara stands on a hillock above the shore not far from Glengorm Castle, or rather, mansion house. Although now completely ruined it was once a very strong position. From here right round the west and south coast of Mull we find many Iron Age forts and defensive positions, where the early settlers stoutly opposed seaborne landings from later incomers, even up to the days of the Vikings.

Just over a mile up the Dervaig road beside the river is the site of the former Mull Combination Poorhouse, with only the lodge now standing. It was built in 1862, a large rambling building designed to accommodate about 170 men and women rendered homeless and destitute as a result of the Clearances.

We continue past the three Mishnish Lochs with their fine angling possibilities, with high on the right the flat-topped hill of 'S Airde Ben (959ft), one of the smaller volcanic necks which extruded some of the local lava flows. There is a little steep-sided crater loch on the top, and from the summit cairn the views to the north and west are outstanding. It is an easy walk to the top by sheep tracks from the old lochs house beside the road.

The wide glen here towards the end of the third loch is called Snake Pass in the English translation, and indeed there is still a fair population of adders to be found. Although not as numerous as in the past, adders can still be seen basking, especially on old walls, in hot sunny weather. They are venomous, of course, but very timid, and vanish at approaching steps. You are advised to carry a stick when walking in any haunt of adders. An adult need fear no more than some slight indisposition for a day if he ever did happen to be bitten — a most rare occurrence — but in the case of a young child it would be wise to consult a doctor.

The road dips down to Loch Torr — an artificial loch — and climbs up the Achnadrish hill, from the top of which one of the best views along the roads of Mull is to be had. This is the second point where the road rises to almost 500 feet. Just past the watershed, there is a boggy hollow below the road where you will see a triangle of three little cairns 30 feet, 30 feet and 45 feet apart, marking, as they say, the leaps taken by an agile MacKinnon clansman when cornered by a raiding party over from the island of Coll, which he outwitted and defeated single-handed. A few hundred yards further on we come to the winding descent to Dervaig village standing at the head of Loch Cumhain. The whole area is steeped in history, with standing stones, stone circles and deserted villages. There is another superlative view from here, this time towards the islands of Coll and Tiree, and in clear weather to the Outer Isles as far as the hills of Harris.

Built by Maclean of Coll about 1800, when he owned much of the north of Mull, Dervaig was originally a street of 26 houses built in pairs with large gardens behind and extensive hill grazings. A new laird — who built Glengorm Castle — tricked the people here out of their hill land when the leases were renewed, causing extreme hardship to a people depending so much on grazing livestock.

Mull had fully its share of the despair and hardships inflicted on its people by lairds of a new era, backed by the indifference of Victorian privilege and a remote central Government. You will come across old drove roads and tracks connecting villages and townships which are now no more than a rickle of stones among the bracken, evidence of a population of 10,000 in the mid 19th century, five times as many as today. In the end little was left but a few farms, struggling crofts and sporting estates. The economy today rests on forestry, cattle and sheep raising, salmon and lobster fishing. Fishing boats are manacled by Common Market regulations and fishing grounds poached by outsiders with impunity. Some clam and scampi fishing has been substituted for some of what has been lost of the islanders' traditional rights.

Dervaig is the most picturesque little village in Mull, noteworthy for the rare design of the 'pencil' steeple of its church. It is something of a centre, with its two shops and Post Office, and offers a wide choice of walks, inland or along the coast. The little salmon river Bellart enters the sea near the village, and many fish gather at the mouth of the burn — it is hardly more — during dry weather. Here you will see a well-preserved example of a salmon trap of the type that was once common at the mouths of rivers and burns frequented by salmon. It is an 'S'-shaped wall of stones built between two headlands over which the fish can swim when it is covered at high tide, and behind which they are often trapped when the tide goes out and the wall becomes a barrier.

Half a mile from the village along the Salen road is the Little Theatre, mentioned earlier, run by Barry and Marianne Hesketh, both professionally-trained in stagecraft. Beyond the bridge a road cuts over the hill for four miles, a short cut to Torloisk, with an ascent of 1:3½ at the summit. On this road, not far from Dervaig, there is the Old Byre, also mentioned earlier, with its tableaux of two houses, one that of an ordinary cottar, the other that of a more prosperous tenant, as they were at the beginning of last century, with a descriptive commentary on tape.

The road winds on through hazel woods to the old mill at Penmore, still with its millwheel. All the estates and some of the larger farms had their own water mills early last century, and there is a place over at Gribun where millstones were cut out and shaped for use in Mull and on the islands. Just beyond Penmore a side road goes to the right for a mile to the tiny haven of Croig, which is still much the same as when cattle from the islands were landed here long ago to be driven through Mull by the old drove roads to Grass Point, opposite Oban, for shipment to the mainland. It is still an unspoilt place with its old slipway and one or two lobster boats. Local sightseeing cruises are catered for, although there is only the old inn by the slipway, now a private dwelling. To the north there are fine views of Ardnamurchan Point, the isle of Rhum and the Small Isles, and the far-off ridge of the Cuillins of Skye. A walk of less than half a mile takes you to a little unsuspected bay of white sand biting into the dark cliffs.

Croig is associated with Calum nan Croig, one of the greatest story-tellers in Mull, who left behind a great store of the most outrageous yarns, long drawn out like all stories in the Gaelic, with the punchline in the last sentence!

Back on the main road, we come to a road leading towards smallholdings and the large farmhouse of Sunipol, where in his early life Thomas Campbell, who later became Poet Laureate, tutored a family. The house is said to be haunted by the ghost of a man who went out from here to Tasmania and who is supposed to have accumulated cash by exploiting the Aborigines and murdering certain of them when doing so, and also by the ghosts of the natives who suffered. Further on, at the end of this road, we see the wild headland of Caliach (Old Woman) where the coastline angles to the south. The old woman after whom the headland is named was once cut off by the tide when she was collecting shellfish, but managed to climb the cliff to safety. Instead of attributing her escape to a benevolent Providence, she boasted of how clever she was in her achievement, and met with an early fate soon afterwards as a punishment for her impiety.

We continue on the main road and see in front of us the wide stretch of Calgary Bay, the showpiece of Mull, whose sandy beach, green machair lands and tree-lined encircling cliffs attract crowds in summer from all over the island. It is overlooked by Calgary House — or Castle — another fine mansion house, but apart from that there are only one or two modernised houses near the bay. A walk along the beach to the north shore brings one to the track leading to the old pier, above which lie the deserted villages of Arin and Innie Vae. The Bay was one of the anchorages from which sailed emigrant ships carrying dispossessed local families from a land that had no use for them, yet who laid the foundations of many thriving British Colonies overseas.

It is incorrect that Calgary, Alberta, in Canada, was named by emigrants from hereabouts. The correct origin lies with Colonel J F Macleod, Commander of the Canadian North-West Mounted Police, a native of Skye. He had spent holidays at Calgary as a guest of the laird, and was so impressed by the atmosphere of the place that in 1876 he asked his host's permission to apply the name to the new fort and settlement he was establishing in Alberta.

Leaving Calgary behind, the road winds along the top of the low cliffs with a sheer drop to the rocks below. This is one of the timed sections of the Tour of Mull Car Rally (which is based in Tobermory) which has to be covered after dark in both directions. The expert driving and incredible times put up over some of the most dangerous and intricate stretches of road can only make the ordinary driver by daylight say, 'It may be true, but I just don't believe it!' At one point, a very sudden and steep descent with a long rockslide above, there is a small flat area below the road and towards the edge of the cliff. It is called Craig a'Chaisteal (Castle Rock) and must have been a place of pre-Christian rites. Two cup-marked rocks stand among the bracken, and some old walling is now almost level with the ground.

Turning inland, the road climbs steadily to a summit cairn from which the whole mountainous centre of Mull, with Ulva's Isle and Loch na Keal, opens out in front, and westwards towards Staffa, Gometra and the Treshnish Islands.

A mile further back just before the ascent, a lonely gaunt ruined building stands up to the right a few hundred yards above the road. This was formerly Reudle Schoolhouse which catered for the scattered communities in this area of Mull, and to which many of the children were obliged to walk for miles to attend. On the walls cut into the plaster are the outlines of old sailing ships, early steamers, and the initials of past generations. The schoolmaster lived in the flat above and his potato drills can still be seen outlined in the heather. Bearing to the right from the building, crossing a drystone wall and keeping to the contour, we come to a wide valley opening out to the south, with the ruins of two deserted villages down below towards the edge of the cliffs. These are Crakaig and Glac-gugairidh (The Hollow of the Dark Grazings), where about 2-300 people once lived. The former has a large communal garden in which grows an old ash tree and is supposed to be haunted by the ghost of a villager who committed suicide by hanging from this tree. The houses — roofless of course — are very well built and are worth studying; probably 18th century.

Descending the steep slopes beyond Crakaig we come to the boulder beach at an inlet where above highwater mark there is a cave of particular interest. The cave is long, straight and dry and at the mouth of it are the foundations of what must have been a very large illicit still, the platform, flue and hollow where the 'black pot' was heated. This still was used up to 1830 until much more severe penalties were imposed on illicit distilling, which in fact was rife in Mull and all over the remoter Highlands. Whisky as a drink was little known in Scotland up to the end of the 17th century; ale was the drink of the people.

The main road descends very steeply indeed for nearly a mile from the cairn and vantage point at the summit from which can be seen the Treshnish Islands. We have referred frequently to these, so perhaps they should be described in more detail at this point.

From Cairnburg Beag in the north, three miles off Treshnish Point, to Bac Mor (Dutchman's Cap) in the south, the Treshnish Islands extend for five miles from north-east to south-west. An arresting stretch of islands, with strange profiles, especially when seen against the unforgettable colours of a Hebridean sunset, they face the open Atlantic, whose strong tides and stormy seas make landings on the exposed shores impossible at times. In spring and early summer they are a nesting place for many species of sea birds which crowd in colonies along the cliffs, while in August they are a breeding place for the grey seal.

The largest island is Lunga, on which are the ruins of several houses where fishermen used to live at certain times of the year. On the west side of Lunga is the rock phenomenon of Dun Cruit (Harp Rock), whose outline from certain angles resembles a Celtic harp. This is a portion of the cliff isolated by a deep-angled cleft, at the bottom of which the waves break and foam continually. Its top is specially favoured by puffins as a nesting place, and in days gone by fishermen used to raid Dun Cruit for eggs and young puffins which were salted down as a winter delicacy. They gained access to the top by carrying the mast of their boat up from the shore and laying it across the abyss, then clambering across with nets to hold the birds and eggs. In spite of the apparent risk, only one man is said to have been lost in the crossing by falling from the mast into the cauldron below.

The northern islands of Cairnburg Mor and Cairnburg Beag were fortified places from before the days of the Vikings; the former, in particular, was an impregnable fortress on top of its ring of cliffs, with any likely access points defended by stout walls. On the top are the ruins of a chapel and a substantial building, used at various times as barracks, fort and prison. Cruises, sometimes with the chance of landing on the islands, are available from centres in Mull.

Towards the foot of the hill we pass a sheep farmhouse and a few other houses, as well as (on the right) the ruins of McArthur's house, which was granted to a man of that name for his services to the Macleans of Torloisk. Just here, if you look west along the coast you will see, about half a mile away, the well-preserved ruins of Dun Aisgean, an Iron Age fort standing on a low eminence above the cliffs. Where the road levels out at the foot of the hill we come to Kilninian Church which was built on the site of a much older building. Outside it, among the tombs, are some very old recumbent grave slabs, two of them possibly those of a chief of the Macleans of Torloisk and his wife. Torloisk is a very scattered community centring on Torloisk House, a mansion house built in the late 18th century replacing an older building. One of the progenitors of the Macleans of Torloisk was Ailean nan Sop, a fierce character who turned pirate and later reformed and returned to his ancestral lands.

We pass the road junction where the short cut from Dervaig comes in, and in three miles arrive at a little glen through which a burn flows in picturesque falls and cataracts, ending in a 90-feet leap over the edge of the cliff just below the road into a pool below on the shore filled by the sea at high tide. A fine view of the falls can be had by descending to the shore by a slope about a quarter of a mile further back and walking along the rocky beach. An interesting fact about the name of the falls is that it is a combination of Gaelic and Scandinavian — Eas Fors (waterfall waterfall).

Another mile takes us to the side road for Ulva Ferry, a short crossing of a few hundred yards to the island of Ulva, and by a rough road through that island to Gometra; both islands are private. However, by telephoning the estate office, anyone genuinely interested is usually readily granted access. The columnar basalts on the south-east of Ulva are spectacular and comparable with the columns of Staffa, resembling in parts the ruins of old buildings; in fact, one part of the shoreline is called The Castles. Ulva has all the evidence of a vanished population in its ruined houses and villages. In 1843 the proprietor boasted about the self-supporting population of 800 and an agricultural economy able to export potatoes. Five years later, hit first by the 1846 potato blight, then by the vicious Clearances and the introduction of sheep by that same laird, there were only 150 people living under restricted conditions near the ferry.

We admit that a reduction in population throughout the Highlands had to come. Settled conditions after the end of the Clan System, sub-division of lands, and a precarious living based too exclusively on a potato economy, led to over-population. The evil of the Clearances was the manner in which they were conducted, the exploitation of the land and its inhabitants by landowners protected by a southern contempt of the Highlanders and a wall of Victorian privilege created by a distant and disinterested Government. One final example of this was a comforting piece of advice given by the aforementioned, much-hated laird of Ulva to tenants he was evicting; he would use his influence to ensure they would be admitted to the Tobermory Poorhouse!

Leaving the road-end for Ulva Ferry, we pass the occasional farmhouse and modernised cottage on the way to the mouth of the River Ba at Killiechronan House (Singing Woods) among its old trees. This is a short and excellent salmon river flowing out of Loch Ba. Looking back along Loch na Keal to the west there are some really arresting views of the great cliffs on the south side of the loch ending in promontories like the outlines of the bows of old-time battleships, rising for 1000 feet to meet the westerly extension of the Ben More massif.

In another mile we arrive at Gruline, where a three-mile road crosses the isthmus to Salen. However, our road lies to the west, along the foot of the mountains and cliffs.

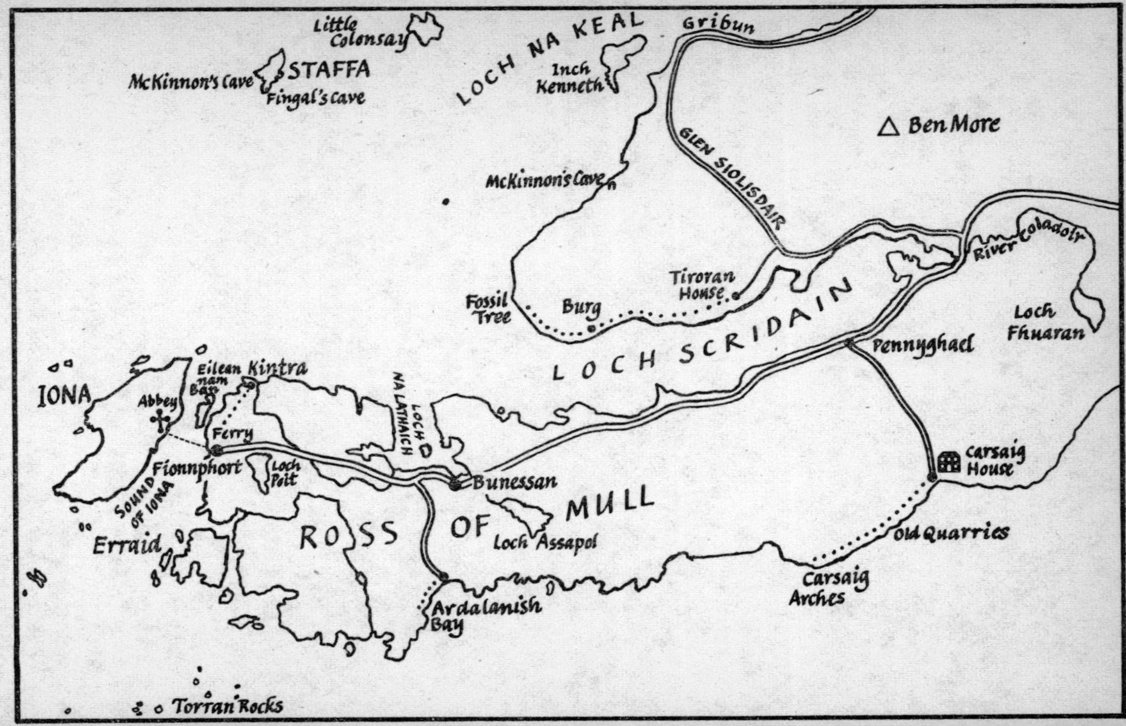
Little Colonsay
STAFFA
McKinnon's Cave
Fingal's Cave
LOCH NA KEAL
Inch Kenneth
Gribun
Ben More
GLEN SIOLISDAIR
McKinnon's Cave
River Coladoir
Loch Fhuaran
Tiroran House
Fossil Tree
Burg
LOCH SCRIDAIN
Pennyghael
IONA
Eilean nam Ban
Kintra
Abbey
Ferry
LOCH NA LATHAICH
Fionnphort
Loch Poit
Bunessan
Carsaig House
SOUND OF IONA
MULL
ROSS
OF
Loch Assapol
Old Quarries
Erraid
Carsaig Arches
Ardalanish Bay
Torran Rocks

Gruline, Gribun, Loch Scridain and the Ross of Mull to Iona Ferry (39 miles)

HALF A MILE FROM THE CROSS-ROADS AT Gruline an avenue leads off to the left to the mausoleum of Lt General Lachlan Macquarie. Governor-General of New South Wales from 1809 to 1820. He retired to this estate which he had acquired and called Jarvisfield, leaving behind a memory as 'Father of Australia' which is remembered to this day. Under the benevolent social activities of his wife the then convict colony of Sydney earned such a favourable reputation back home in Britain that some despairing people committed crimes which would ensure their transportation there. Much exploration was carried out by the General as far south as Tasmania, and many place names from Mull are to be found there which were bestowed by him. He and his family are buried in the mausoleum within the little enclosure at Gruline.

With Gruline, Knock and Ben More Lodge so near each other, this was and still is a centre for stalking among the Ben More hills and angling on Loch Ba. This attractive loch is Mull's second largest, extending for two miles into the heart of the mountains where lie the much-eroded volcanic centres from which vast outpourings of lava created a mountain — once 8000 feet high — and the general landscape of Mull. Hill paths, rights of way and short cuts for people in days long past, attract walkers nowadays by Loch Ba over the passes connecting with roads on the south side of the island. Four miles from the narrow bridge at Gruline, at the isolated farm of Dishaig, the easy ascent of Ben More (3169ft) begins. From the summit of the mountain (which is the highest accumulation of Tertiary lavas in Britain, as well as the only 'Munro' in the Hebrides outside the Isle of Skye) the views are unsurpassed in clear weather.

Beyond Dishaig the road suddenly turns a corner into a grim world of rocks, with crumbling cliffs towering above to 1000 feet and a drop of 50 feet to the sea below. This is a gloomy dangerous half mile of road which travellers are glad to leave behind when the cliffs draw back and a few houses, some fertile fields and a couple of little farms appear. This is Gribun.

Just opposite a clump of wind-blown trees at the first farmhouse you come to, beside the road there is an enormous boulder, a relic of the rock avalanches that have fallen over the ages. It is a monument to a sad event that took place at the end of the 18th century. A young shepherd from the Ross of Mull had arranged to marry a local girl. On the night of the wedding, when the celebrations were being held in the farm steading and house opposite, the young couple slipped away to the tiny cot house which stood safely on the other side of the road protected from rockfalls by the great rock that stood above it. That very night this rock split, part of it rolling down for 50 feet or so, coming to rest on the very top of the cot house which it crushed to extinction along with its two occupants, who were never seen again. Up to the end of last century a few of the wooden rafter could still be seen projecting under the rock. Now a little wall and a few flowers mark the spot where the young couple perished so tragically.

Just beyond, a track leads down to the slipway for the crossing to the island of Inch Kenneth, called after a disciple of St Columba, an island second in sanctity to Iona in early days. There is a ruined chapel there, many gravestones, a small farmhouse and the mansion house. Access to the island is discouraged. Not far from the slipway at Gribun, at the west end of an old fence, is a flat stretch of hard grey sandstone where millstones used to be cut and shaped. One still lies half cut out of the rock.

Beyond the second farm, which lies on the flat lands before the road begins the ascent from Gribun, a marked path through the fields takes us to MacKinnon's Cave, which is reached through a gate in the fence protecting the edge of the cliff. A sharp descent is followed by a 300-yards scramble along the boulders to where a tiny waterfall comes down almost at the entrance to the cave, whose entrance is so vast that Dr Johnson and Boswell were greatly impressed when they visited it during their tour of Mull. It is partly cut off at high tide, so visit it on a half and falling tide. It extends for a considerable distance into total darkness — remember to take a good torch with you — until blocked by rockfalls just beyond a great cavern, in the centre of which is a flat table-like rock called 'Fingal's' or 'MacKinnon's' Table. The cave was called after the Abbot MacKinnon, whose tomb is in Iona Cathedral, who made this his cell for a time. He appreciated the silence after moving from Staffa where the roar of the sea disturbed his meditations.

There is a story of a party who, led by a piper, set out to explore the cave. Others listening above were to mark the line of the cave. Presently, however, they heard the piper change to a new tune — 'Would that I had three hands, two for the pipes and one for the sword' — after which the music became discordant and finally stopped. The others armed themselves, lit bright torches and entered the cave. They came across the body of the piper first. He had charmed the evil spirits of the cave with his music as long as he could keep playing; the others were found killed and mutilated further in. Later, a dog which had accompanied the exploring party emerged from the other side of the headland with every hair burned off its body. The atmosphere of the cave, if not the memory of this old tale, make one relieved to emerge again into the daylight.

Before we leave Loch na Keal behind us, mention should be made of that other natural curiosity, the island of Staffa, that lies off Loch na Keal towards the Treshnish Islands. Its name, which means 'Pillar Island', graphically describes its appearance. A mile long by a quarter of a mile wide, it slopes gently downwards from the cave-indented southern end to its northern tip. The caves of Staffa are famous, most particularly Fingal's Cave, whose Gaelic name *An Uamh Fine* meant 'Melodious Cave', and whose echoing surge of the waves inspired Mendelssohn's well-known overture. Staffa was little known, and then only locally, until 1772, when Sir Joseph Banks heard of it when his ship put in for shelter to the Isle of Mull. In 1847 Queen Victoria and Prince Albert were two famous visitors who were greatly impressed. As in the case of the Treshnish Islands, cruises to visit the island and land there if weather permits can be arranged locally in Mull.

Leaving this spectacular region of wild cliffs, rocks and folklore, continue down the straight length of Glen Siolisdair (Iris Glen) with its young forestry plantations, looking south across Loch Scridain to the Ross of Mull. We reach the seashore at the Church of Kilfinichen, from which we can strike west and explore the high wild headland of Ardmeanach and Burg. A side road leads along the head of the little bay to Tiroran House in its sun-trap of sheltering trees; the explorer should leave his car — if that is how he is travelling — at the end of the wood beyond, where a small burn flows across the road and the track degenerates and rises steeply. In about three miles we pass the farm of Tavool, and shortly afterwards, along the farm track, we come to the end of the road — the sheep farm of Burg, where the visitor should report his intention of proceeding further, for this is now National Trust Property, appropriately called 'The Wilderness'.

From there it is a stiff but exhilarating walk of two miles or so, first by farm track, then by sheep and wild goat tracks along the foot of the towering 1000-foot cliffs, with the steep slope to the rocks below, to the site of MacCulloch's famous Fossil Tree, discovered by MacCulloch, the geologist, in 1819. The descent to the boulder beach is made down a grassy glissade at a point from where fantastic shapes of columnar basalts are seen cut out on the rocks below, then continue for half a mile along the rocks to the second (northern) waterfall pouring over the edge of the cliff. The Tree, one of the wonders of Europe, stands in a recess above highwater mark about 100 yards beyond the waterfall. It is the impression of an ancient 40-foot pine tree which was one of many covered over by the earliest flow of lava, now eroded back to a point where the tree is exposed in cross-section, with the five-foot fossilised foot of the trunk still preserved. Even the grain of the wood has been preserved in stone, and in a cavity behind the trunk some of the original carbon is still preserved after probably 40-50 million years. The columnar basalts round the Tree and along this length of coast are fantastic. A word of advice again — explore at half tide on a falling tide or you risk perhaps being cut off for hours.

Having returned to Burg farmhouse, the energetic explorer goes back to Tiroran and continues along the main road under the slopes of Ben More, past the ice-scored rocks at the edge of Loch Scridain, to join the new main road from Glen More where it crosses the River Coladoir at the head of Loch Scridain near Kinloch Inn. Three miles from the cross-roads, heading for Iona, just beyond the hamlet of Pennyghael, a road climbs for four miles over the moorlands to Carsaig, and the sudden descent comes as a surprise as the road dips steeply through tall trees past Carsaig House to end at the pier referred to by Dr Johnson as a link with the mainland south of Oban. There is a residential school of painting at Carsaig House: and where in the whole country could there be a finer or more inspiring setting? The wide green fields lie in an amphitheatre of 700-foot cliffs down which many waterfalls pour like white veils in rainy weather towards the curving beach of dark basalt sand with offshore reefs. Eastwards a bridle path skirts the shore for six miles to Lochbuie, which will be described later.

Rounding the bay under the bold headland a rough walk takes us in about a mile, following highwater mark below the cliffs, to the Nuns' Cave, which lies just short of another picturesque waterfall. On the west wall of this wide, shallow cave are ancient designs of crosses, roses etc inscribed by the monks of Iona, who used the cave as a shelter and workshop while carving the hard grey sandstones prised from the horizontal layers in the tidal quarry on the shore in front. This ornamental stonework was used in the building of Iona Cathedral, for grave slabs, and so on. Another mile and a half takes the energetic walker to the famous Carsaig Arches, tunnels and arches cut by the sea through columnar basalts. Care must be taken when exploring them as there are dangerous paths and steps among the rocks. Just short of the Nuns' Cave there is a thick layer of worn sandstones packed with fossil mussel and other shells, for this is a raised portion of the ancient land platform on which the lavas of Mull were piled up.

Back over the hill to the main road and a quarter of a mile beyond the isolated church just above the shore is a railed-off cairn surmounted by a small rough stone cross. This was erected to the memory of the Beaton doctors, who up to the eighteenth century were physicians renowned throughout the islands for their knowledge of herbal remedies inherited from the monks of Iona. Their fame even reached the Royal Court in Edinburgh, where the King, James VI, convened a meeting of all the greatest doctors in Scotland and set them a test to decide who was the greatest of them all. One of the Beaton doctors emerged triumphantly from the test; but jealous of his success the other doctors succeeded in administering a poison which led to his death, for they took the precaution of hiding all the antidotes for which the expiring doctor called. The cross is to his memory, and the initials GMB 1582 DMB, now worn away, were carved on the base of it; these were the initials of the two most famous Beatons. The family came originally from Béthune in France — hence the name. They settled for a time near Pennyghael, where they had an enclosure where their medicinal herbs were grown.

Another, more modern, cairn stands above a straight section of the road just short of the village of Bunessan. It was erected to the memory of Mary MacDonald, a local woman who could not read or write, yet who composed that lovely hymn known to us as *Child in the Manger*.

Bunessan is a busy, cheerful little place at the head of a shallow sea loch, with a pier that used to be a regular calling place for MacBrayne's coasting ships. There is quite a social life here all the year round. Like Tobermory and other lesser townships in Mull, there is no lack of things to do during the winter time. It is an excellent centre for exploring the neighbourhood — sandy bays like Ardalanish; fossil leaf-beds at the headland of Ardtun; the ancient chapel of Kilviceon; standing stones and many coastal forts. The landscape of this end of the Ross of Mull differs from the rest of the island. It consists of pre-Tertiary granites, low hills, fertile fields and many scattered crofts and farms — the main crofting district of Mull.

The end of the road and ferry for Iona, 50 miles by main road from Tobermory, is at Fionnphort (White Port) five miles from Bunessan. Like that village, Fionnphort is another good centre for exploring around. Kintra, a mile or two to the north, is a counterpart of Croig in the north of Mull, a little haven where cattle were landed from the islands. Less than a mile to the north are the Tormore granite quarries, where there are still stockpiles of large blocks of red or pink granite abandoned when the workings closed down at the beginning of the century. For many years there was a thriving industry here in extracting and shaping the lovely pinkish granite for export, chiefly to America, from a little pier in the sandy bay known as the 'Bullhole' that lies below. The quarry was connected to the pier by a tramway whose course can still be seen. A favourite anchorage for yachtsmen, the 'Bullhole' is protected by the island of Eilean nam Ban (Women's Island) to which St Columba banished all the women from Iona during his lifetime; for as he said (a Gaelic quotation still current in Mull), 'Where there is a cow there is a woman; and where there is a woman there is mischief!' So the humble cow had to share exile from Iona. The ruins of very old houses can still be seen on Women's Island.

South of Fionnphort lies the tidal island of Erraid featured in Stevenson's *Kidnapped.* Until recently it was a lighthouse shore station. This part of Mull was known to RLS, for his uncle was the contractor based here during the building of the lighthouses of Skerryvore (off Tiree) and Ardnamurchan. South of Erraid lie the Torran (Thunder) Rocks, an area of dangerous reefs where during stormy weather the roar of the waves can be heard miles away.

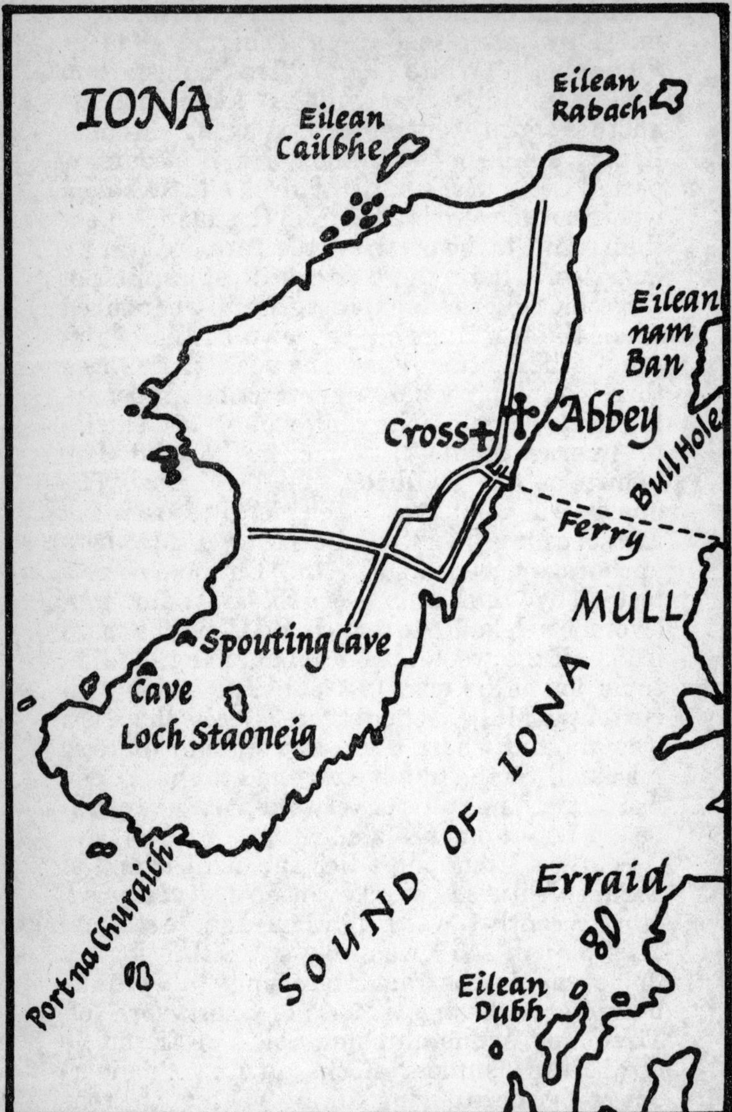
IONA
Eilean Cailbhe
Eilean Rabach
Eilean nam Ban
Cross
Abbey
Bull Hole
Ferry
MULL
Spouting Cave
Cave
Loch Staoneig
SOUND OF IONA
Port na Churaich
Erraid
Eilean Dubh

Iona

THE LITTLE ISLAND OF IONA, THREE miles long by one and a half miles wide, is divided from Mull by the mile-wide Sound of Iona, across which a regular ferry runs from the slipway at Fionnphort. This is an artist's paradise, with green translucent waters, blue reflections, pink rocks, white sands, backed by the green machair. So much is known and has been written about Iona that there is little need to go into details which the explorer will discover for himself when he sets foot on the island.

One basic question that arises is — why did Columba, an influential churchman, a Prince of Ireland, descended from Niall of the Nine Hostages, High King of Ireland, renounce his heritage and voluntarily exile himself for ever, and settle in what was a Druid-ridden pagan environment? He was not prompted entirely by a missionary-urge to spread the gospel, although in doing so he was highly successful, and centuries later he was to be referred to as the 'Morning Star of Scotland's Faith'.

What happened was this: Columba was always critical of the over-strict orthodoxy of the Church, which he believed lacked the appeal of simplicity for ordinary people. Therefore, when he heard that the abbot Finnian had brought back with him from Rome a new and simplified translation of the Gospels, Columba was naturally keen to obtain a copy, but this was refused. Not to be outdone, he secretly borrowed the script, but was discovered when making a copy of it for his private use. He refused to give up either his copy or the notes, even when ordered to do so by the High King of Ireland, who pronounced that famous verdict on copyright: 'To every cow its calf, and to every book its copy'. Columba was thus guilty of the first recorded breach of copyright.

In the end the two sides took up arms in support of their principles. On the one side were the supporters of strict orthodoxy, and on the other Columba's party seeking to present a more easily understood interpretation of the Scriptures. Later, in Iona, Columba was to set up the Church of the Culdees (Servants of God) throughout the land under the disapproving eye of the parent church, which finally disbanded the Culdees in the 12th century. Anyway, in the battle which followed, Columba's side prevailed, but only after great slaughter, which so preyed on his mind that as a self-imposed penance he left Ireland for ever.

Landing first on the island of Oronsay, an islet joined at low tide to Colonsay, he found he could still see the distant hills of Ireland, so he moved on again to the north-west, where he came ashore at what is called the Port of the Coracle on the south side. He could not discern the shores of Ireland from the highest point of

Iona, Dun-i (332ft) so here he settled. The coracle in which he travelled is supposed to have been buried beneath a mound in case Columba might be tempted to give up his penance and return to Ireland. Some of those coracles were large seaworthy frameworks of wood and wattles covered with hides and waterproofed with pitch and tallow, which could sail well enough in a favouring wind.

Iona came to be called by many names, among them *I-Chaluim Chille* or Island of the Cell of Columba. At first he had to overcome the pagan practices of Druidical priests. As time went on Columba and his disciples became established not as cloistered clerics, but as militant monks, skilled in the arts of farming, building, medicine, and the beautifying of written records — the *Book of Kells*, for instance, the most beautiful book in the world, still preserved in Ireland. Many of those accomplishments were passed on to the people and preserved through the Dark Ages.

Thanks to the gradual inter-mixing of the Celts and Picts, Columba was able to preach and talk to the Pictish peoples in a language they could understand, and whom in time he won over to Christianity. Monks from Iona established Lindisfarne and their influence reached across the North Sea to the Low Countries, and even far up the Rhine.

Pilgrims came to Iona from far distances, in fact, another title earned by this monastic centre was the 'University of the North'. From the point nearest Oban all the way through the Ross of Mull there were standing stones, a few of which survive, to guide travellers along the Pilgrim's Way, as well as the funeral cortèges which so often followed the same route instead of sailing round the south of Mull.

Geologically, Iona is quite different from the rest of Mull, and is formed of some of the oldest and most stable rocks in the world. It is strange how this comparative permanence seemed to be known instinctively long ago, and has come down to us in an old Gaelic proverb stating that when all the islands round about were submerged, Iona would stand proudly above the waves. This is partly the reason why 48 Scottish kings, and others from Norway, Ireland and France, together with many great dignitaries and clan chiefs, were interred here in Reilig Oran, the oldest Christian burying place in Scotland. Here lies MacBeth, killed in 1057, and Duncan, whom he murdered in 1040, their bodies, if not their spirits, united in death. However, Shakespeare drew heavily on his imagination to depict MacBeth as the villain and Duncan the stainless Royal image, whereas history reverses their characters. On both counts — permanence and sanctity — interment in Iona was sought by the great both far and near.

Iona suffered severely when it was sacked three times between 795 and 986 by the roving Vikings; yet even at worst a certain superstitious reticence kept the raiders from permanently extinguishing this candle of Christianity. By the 11th century the Vikings had become Christianised, and 100 years later the Bishop of Iona was being elected at Trondjem in Norway. The final destruction of Iona was a result of the bigotry of the 16th-century Reformers. In their misplaced zeal they destroyed irreplaceable relics and records going back to the days of St Columba; 365 beautifully-carved crosses were smashed, thrown into the sea, or taken away, as also were the bells of the cathedral. The monks were expelled in 1561, but the nuns were left until 1574, when the island of Iona came into the hands of the Macleans of Duart.

The fleeing monks were able to save a few of the old records which ultimately found a home in the archives of the Vatican, in Paris, and in Ireland. It is said that the monks hid some of the records on the Treshnish Island of Cairnburg Mor, but they were discovered and destroyed by Cromwell's men. It would be a wonderful find to come across traces of those old records missed by the searchers! The nuns sheltered in Nuns' Cave, Carsaig, hence its name.

The Duke of Argyll finally took over ownership of Iona from the Macleans in the 17th century. In 1899, George, 8th Duke of Argyll, gave the ruined buildings in trust to the Church of Scotland, on condition that they were to be interdenominational. Then in 1938 the Very Rev Dr George F MacLeod gave up his charge and came to Iona, where he founded the Iona Community, a group of Christian students, workers and worshippers, who began the restoration of the old Abbey buildings with stonework salvaged from old unidentified ruins. Support came from all over the world, and now the buildings have been restored to something of their old grandeur. In recognition of his devoted services Dr MacLeod was granted the title of Lord MacLeod of Fuinary.

No visitor can fail to feel that Iona has an 'atmosphere' all of its own, as if something intangible of St Columba still holds the island. The intervening span of 1400 years could well be no more than a century, so vivid are the impressions.

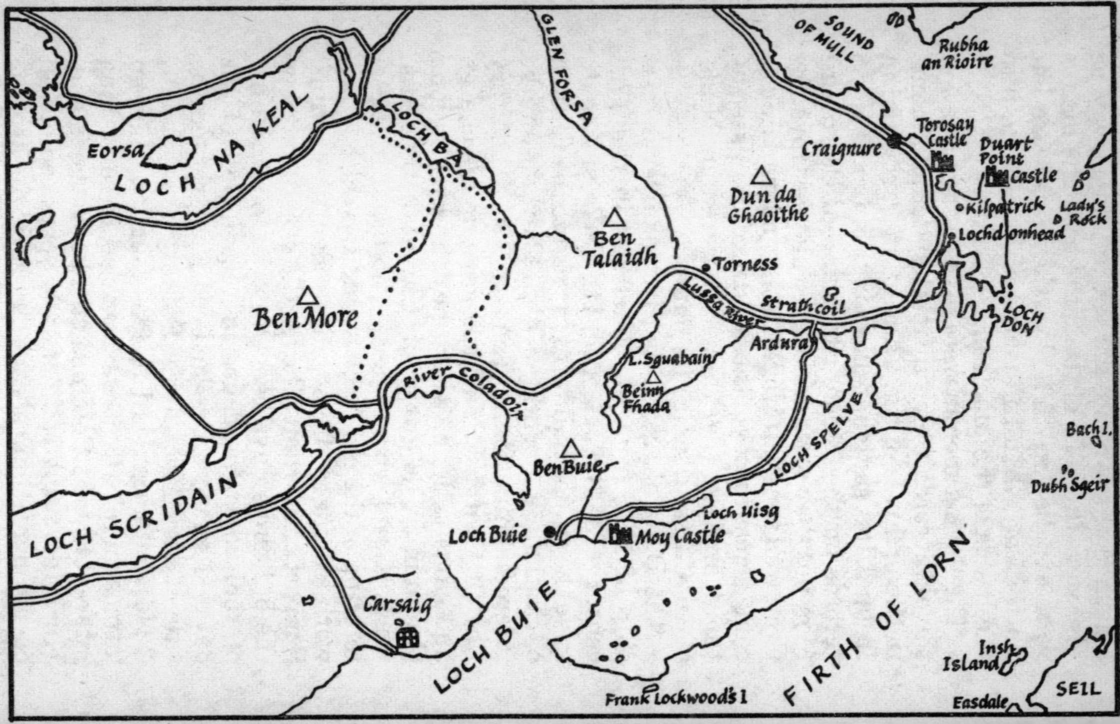

SOUND OF MULL
Rubha an Rioire
GLEN FORSA
LOCH NA KEAL
Eorsa
LOCH BA
Torosay Castle
Craignure
Duart Point
Castle
Lady's Rock
Kilpatrick
Lochdonhead
Dun da Ghaoithe
Ben Talaidh
Torness
Ben More
Strathcoil
Lussa River
LOCH DON
Ardura
L. Sguabain
Beinn Fhada
River Coladoir
Bach I.
LOCH SPELVE
Ben Buie
Dubh Sgeir
LOCH SCRIDAIN
Loch Uisg
Loch Buie
Moy Castle
FIRTH OF LORN
Carsaig
LOCH BUIE
Insh Island
Frank Lockwood's I
SEIL
Easdale

Glen More, Lochbuie and Duart to Craignure (42 miles from Fionnphort)

LEAVING BEHIND IONA AND ALL ITS memories, we retrace our steps to Kinloch. Then at the head of Loch Scridain at the cross-roads where we came in from the west we keep straight on by the new road into Glen More. To begin with, Glen More is wide, flat and boggy, with peat mosses covering great boulders and stone slabs which can be seen exposed in the bed of the River Coladoir. At the new bridge near the cross-roads there is a highly photogenic pool in the river with the background of the Glen More mountains.

A mile or two up the road, the hill path from Loch Ba, crossing the shoulder of Ben More, comes down the hillside on the left beside a sheep fank. On the opposite side of the road a cart track heads for a ford across the Coladoir and continues for a mile to the ruined farm-house of Derrynaculen, a two-storey building looking across the glen to the changing aspects of Ben More. There are extensive sheep fanks behind, where a tall waterfall drops through a deep cleft in the precipitous hill face. An enclosed garden and flat fields of good land complete the picture of the dwelling which was the birthplace of the Mull bard, Dugald MacPhail, Dughall an t'Strath Chaoil (Dugald of Strath Coil). He was the composer of that beautiful air which is the anthem of Mull, *The Isle of Mull*, composed when he was far away in employment in Newcastle. He was brought up in and loved the other end of the glen — Strath Coil — and there, at Ardura, stands the cairn built to his memory in the 1920s with stones carted from Derrynaculen. He lived from 1818 to 1887.

The glen narrows as the road climbs past the last building, the isolated dwelling house of Craig, up to the watershed at nearly 700 feet. Here you will see excellent examples of glaciation, for a local glacier once filled the glen, leaving isolated boulders, moraine heaps and scarred rock faces as evidence of its flow, recession and final melting. When the new road was being built many problems were faced in excavating, filling in deep peat holes and blasting rocky outcrops. At least there was no lack of rock materials.

Surely in all Scotland there is no glen with such a store of folklore and traditions, and we are in the heart of it here where the road begins to dip down towards Strath Coil and Loch Spelve. Down below you will see a chain of three small lochs curving towards the south along the bottom of a side glen towards Lochbuie. The left-hand loch is called Loch Sguabain, and from it the busy bustling little River Lussa flows for five or six miles down Strath Coil to a fine sea-pool where it flows into Loch Spelve. The Lussa is a good little salmon river when conditions are right, for which permits to fish may be had from Torosay Estate. If you halt above the lochs and take a stroll for a couple of hundred yards down to the old road, you will see a lay-by beside which stands a great pointed boulder. This is Clach Sguabain (Sguabain's Rock).

Sguabain was one of the giants of Fingal. One day, as he was standing here ruminating, he saw Nicol, one of his fellow giants, also standing beyond the intervening hills over on the shore of Loch Spelve. After all, none of these hills exceeds 2300 feet in height! For some reason a quarrel developed and they began to hurl abuse at each other. In the end Nicol angrily plucked up a boulder and hurled it at Sguabain, where it stands to this day. Not to be outdone, Sguabain retaliated by tearing out an equally formidable rock and tossed it at Nicol, and you can see it as well lying on the shore of Loch Spelve. Their aim appears to have been poor, for no record of personal injury has come down.

Now look down to Loch Sguabain and you will see towards the eastern end a little islet; it may have been a crannog, that is, an artificial island, of which there were several in the Mull lochs. Back in the 16th century this was the island-fortress-home of Eoghann (Ewen) a'Chinn Bhig, son and heir of the old fifth chief of the MacLaines of Lochbuie, who was married to a greedy grasping MacDougall wife, who pestered him to ask for more and more land from his patient father. However, in the end Lochbuie refused a further request, and goaded into action, Ewen threatened to take land by force. His father was adamant and the result was an armed confrontation between father, aided by his brother, Maclean of Duart, and Ewen and his followers on a flat piece of land between Craig and Loch Sguabain, probably somewhere near the watershed.

Back in those days a fight of this nature used to be rather like a duel, the principals agreeing on a time and place in advance. The day before the fight, as Ewen was riding past a little burn, he saw a little woman in green — obviously a fairy — busy washing clothes. Drawing up, he enquired with that respect which is always due to the Little People if she could foretell the outcome of the coming fight. Her strange reply was that next morning, if he had to ask for butter to be set on the table at the first meal of the day, he would lose the fight. Riding on, he forgot all about the prophecy, until at the breakfast table he found the servant girl had forgotten to lay butter on the board, and as he called for it, he recalled the grim warning.

However, he led his men bravely into the attack, and a bitter struggle ensued; until a henchman of the old chief's caught Ewen at a disadvantage, and with a sweep of his broad-sword cut his head clean off his shoulders, thus ending the fight and fulfilling the prophecy. Jammed in the stirrups, Ewen's headless body was carried from the battlefield by his maddened charger for the intervening miles to the ford across the Lussa, just above the falls. Slowed up by the stiff climb on the other side the steed came to a trembling halt and Ewen's body fell to the ground. To mark the spot his followers erected a little cairn — we shall come to the exact spot further along the glen.

Since then the headless ghost of Ewen of the Little Head, riding his black charger, has haunted the roads of Mull, and has even been known to fly over to the island of Coll. When a member of the House of Lochbuie was on the point of death, the ghost was known to ride furiously around old Moy Castle at Lochbuie.

Even Sir Walter Scott knew of the apparition when he wrote these lines in his *Lady of the Lake*:

Sounds, too, had come in midnight blast
Of charging steed, careering fast
Along Ben Talla's shingly side,
Where mortal horseman ne'er might ride.

Ben Talla — or Talaidh — sometimes called the 'Sugar Loaf' because of its symmetrical shape, is that isolated mountain between the angle of Glen More and the head of Glen Forsa.

Many tales are told in Mull about Ewen a'Chinn Bhig. For instance, as you are walking along the shore of Loch Ba along the path that leads over to Glen More, you will see the gnarled trunk of a large tree lying almost horizontal a few yards from the path among younger trees. One night a Maclean man from Duart was walking here when he was confronted by the Headless Horseman, who attacked him. Grasping a young sapling with one hand, he desperately fought off the ghost with his dirk held in the other hand. Neither could prevail until cockcrow, which of course is the sign which drives apparitions away to their daylight haunts; reluctantly Ewen faded away, leaving the Maclean man to tell the tale; but so desperate had been the fight that he had almost pulled the sapling out by the roots, and in that position it grew over the years. Of course, the fact that almost all modern sightings occur after closing time may be no more than a coincidence!

Returning again to Clach Sguabain, just look across the loch to the ridge of the hill that rises above it to the south. This is Ben Fhada (1603ft) or the Long Hill. If you care to walk down past the stalkers' and shepherds' bothy at Ishriff and climb to the top of the hill, you will see a long hollow on the summit. This was worn by the long scaly body of a fearsome dragon which had its lair here, from which it descended to terrorise the glen. Wayfarers and livestock vanished down its fiery maw and the glen became shunned by all, so much so that the local king — there were many little kings in the land in those days — in desperation offered half his kingdom and the hand of his becoming daughter to anyone who would rid him of this importunate beast. Knights, and soldiers armed to the teeth sought it out, but were never seen again.

However, one day a little ship anchored at the head of Loch Scridain and a young man began to construct a floating causeway of barrels between ship and shore, driving long sharp spikes into the barrels. He then landed a herd of cattle beasts which he began to drive up the glen, prodding them with his *sgian dubh* (black knife) which was his only weapon. Once over the watershed they came in sight of the dragon, which was peering expectantly from the top of the hill. Drooling at the chops at the sight of so much food it came bounding down, past Loch Sguabain, breathing fire and smoke like all good dragons.

At once the young man turned the herd and began to urge it back along the road it had come — not that it needed much encouragement. When the breath of the overtaking beast was hot on his back the man dispatched one of the cattle, the devouring of which delayed the dragon for a space. With the beast leaping close behind again, the sacrifice of another beast gave the rest of the herd yet another breathing space — and so on all the way back to Loch Scridain, where by this time only a single member of the herd was left, whose demise delayed the dragon just long enough for the young man to dodge his way out to the ship between the spikes of the floating barrels. Angered by the escape of the last of his prey the dragon began to clamber precariously along the barrels; but impaled first by one spike, then by another, it became helplessly entangled, and it was easy for the ingenious young man to dispatch it with a borrowed axe. So he up-anchored and sailed away to the haven in front of the king's castle, towing the evidence of the dead dragon. The young man duly received half the kingdom and the hand of the glamorous princess, and they lived happily ever after, as all the best stories finish!

Surfeited with superstition and filled with folklore, the explorer takes to the road again, round the right-angled bend where Glen More turns abruptly south into Strath Coil. The walker can cut north here past the foot of Ben Talaidh and down Glen Forsa to the Sound of Mull. Just at the point where the road passes the ruined houses at Torness, draw up, and take the path going down to the river beside the most westerly of the ruins. After only 100 yards it forks, the right-hand taking you to the ford and foot bridge, the left to the Falls of Lussa. A further 100 yards along the right-hand path, just before the descent, you will see in the heather the tiny cairn marking where the headless body of Eoghann a'Chinn Bhig fell from his exhausted charger. You must also explore the nearby Falls of Lussa, a lovely gorge with a pool of clear water where the angler will usually be thrilled by the sight of salmon and seatrout resting in the holding places.

Through woods of oak and holly and the green plantations of the Forestry Commission, we come to the crossroads at Ardura, not far from the long sea pool where the Lussa flows along the flats into Loch Spelve. Beside the intersection stands the four-square monument to Dugald MacPhail mentioned earlier. Each of the panels is inscribed with a verse in Gaelic from his lovely composition *The Isle of Mull.*

The new road has been constructed at a level higher up the slopes of Strath Coil, and there is a delightful quiet walk up the old road which goes through the woods keeping close to the River Lussa. Along this walk about two miles from Ardura the road climbs round a low bluff above an attractive salmon pool called the Pedlar's Pool. On the low bank here among the thick bracken you will see a cairn surmounted by an iron cross of Celtic design with the words 'John Jones, Died 1 April 1891'.

This John Jones was a pedlar who roamed the roads with his pack. In the course of his rounds he arrived at a house in the Ross of Mull where the occupants were lying desperately ill with smallpox. Cases of this disease still cropped up at the end of last century, and it was regarded with almost superstitious horror by the people, who often refused to go near the victims, leaving food and necessities near the infected house to be collected by the occupants if they were able to do so. Anyway, this brave pedlar stayed at the house tending the victims of the disease until it had run its course, whereupon he shouldered his pack and set out again to take the road. Unfortunately, when he arrived at this lovely spot beside the Lussa he found himself overtaken by such a virulent attack of smallpox that he collapsed and died, unknown and unheeded. His body was found later and interred there with his pack, and subsequently the cairn was erected to his memory.

At Ardura take the road over the steep Ardura hill for the eight miles to Lochbuie. At the top of the ascent there is a seat and 'wishing well' that were erected to remind the weary traveller of a local benefactress, Margaret Elliot, who died in 1924. Continue to Loch Uisg among its rhododendrons and pine trees, more like a sheltered corner of the Trossachs than a corner of a wind-swept Hebridean island. The road reaches the pebbly shore of Loch Buie, open to the Atlantic, beside a pyramidical monument erected to commemorate the coronation of King Edward VII by 'Lochbuie and his Highlanders'. This, of course, was formerly the land of the Maclaines of Lochbuie, who were descended from the Macleans of Duart through the fourth chief. The estate became heavily mortgaged and was foreclosed and lost to the Maclaines early in the present century. A rough road continues to the right along the shore as far as Glenbyre, then by a pathway to Carsaig.

Moy Castle with the modern mansion house close by stands on the rocks above the shore less than a mile along to the left. Because of the dangerous condition of some of the stonework, access to the castle is no longer permitted. It is a square tower-house of three storeys, with a dungeon and a well in the floor of the kitchen which refills to a fixed level as fast as it is emptied. It is not a strong defensive position, but is highly convenient to the shore, where the rocks were cleared to afford a channel for the easy handling of galleys.

Behind the castle is a little plain, or *Magh* as it is called in Gaelic, from which the name 'Moy' is derived, on which are standing stones and Mull's best-preserved example of a stone circle. The rough Laggan peninsula, where there are many herds of red deer, lies to the east. At the southern end of the peninsula lies Lord Lovat's Cave, an intricate cave at different levels where Lord Lovat is supposed to have hidden during the troubled times.

Lochbuie is dominated to the north by the high bulk of Ben Buie (2354ft). This reminds me of one of the many stories told by that masterly raconteur, Calum nan Croig, already mentioned in connection with Croig, in the north of Mull. He and his wife were living at the time in a cottage at the very foot of Ben Buie. As he said, he was 'getting on', in other words, he was no longer in his prime. There had been a heavy snowstorm that left the Ben with a heavy coating. Calum's wife had decided to go away for the day to visit someone — anyway, he was left on his own. 'So', said Calum, 'I thought I would see if I could still climb to the top of the Ben the way I used to do when I was a young man. Well, I got on fine, and reached the top. Now, I thought, I'll try and roll a big snowball the way I did when I was a boy. So I started it small and it got bigger and bigger with the soft snow, until I could hardly roll it, and then I managed to roll it over the edge . . .'

Away went the snowball rolling down the slopes out of sight, picking up snow and things as it went until it was far bigger than a house — and it still had a long way to go to reach the foot.

'I began to go back home down the hill' continued Calum. 'When I reached the foot there was nothing to see but great piles of snow; not a sign of our house, so I got a spade and began to dig. After a bit I came across a big stag picked up by the snowball; then another; then three sheep; more deer and sheep, and lots of rabbits. Well, by the time I dug out our house I had one heap of 34 deer, another with 99 sheep, and 143 rabbits I hid at the side.' He reported the find of deer and sheep to the keeper, then returned home, where his wife was waiting. He told her all about it and how he had reported his potential larder to the keeper. 'But I never told her about the rabbits. I sold them later and kept the money for myself.'

'My!' she accused him, 'Are you not the great fool. Could you no' have kept something for yourself; and 99 sheep . . .' she added sarcastically . . . Could you no' have made it the even 100?'

'Ach, be quiet, woman', retorted Calum indignantly, 'Would you be making me a liar for the sake of one sheep?'

Of course, in the original Gaelic this story spins out for half an evening, with many asides. It was not so much the merit of the stories told at the ceilidhs, but the gifted manner in which they were delivered that captivated the audiences.

Leaving Moy Castle and Lochbuie behind us — and many are the tales from the past told about the castle, and how it changed hands — we return by the Ardura hill to the main road heading for Craignure. Just before the tiny hamlet of Lochdonhead whose row of houses straggles round the head of the shallow loch, a narrow road branches to the right, crossing an inlet of Loch Don by a narrow, single-span, high-arched bridge built late in the 18th century, about the same time as Aros Bridge was erected at Salen, and in about three miles reaches the pier at Grass Point. This is the nearest point of Mull to the mainland at Oban and was an important place in the past when all the cattle from Mull and the neighbouring islands had to pass through it for shipment over to Kerrera and Oban to continue their long trek to the markets of the south. There is a substantial jetty from which cruises are available, and private communications with Oban. The old inn is now a private house, with a tea-room and a museum, and the owner has placed some realistic models of seals on the rocks in front.

There are other smaller landing places along this stretch of coast from which tracks used to run towards the Ross of Mull. These were used long ago for funeral parties conveying the bodies of great men who were to be interred in the sacred soil of Iona.

Back to Lochdonhead and continuing along the main road, we come to a signpost pointing to Kilpatrick, where the approach road to Duart branches to the right, and the castle is seen about a mile away standing on its strong eminence above the shore. Apart from its defensive position — the flatter approach from inland was protected by an artificial ditch — it commanded the Sound of Mull, Loch Linnhe and the Firth of Lorne. The castle buildings were extended from time to time. The oldest part of the building dates from the 13th century, and like Aros Castle it originally belonged to the MacDougalls of Lorne, who owned Mull before they fell from power and were succeeded by the Lords of the Isles.

The founder of the Clan Maclean was Lachlan, who by marrying a daughter of the Lord of the Isles was given generous lands in Mull. The clan followed the Lords of the Isles, when they in turn fell from grace, as the most powerful clan in the southern Hebrides.

Weakened by their support of Montrose and the Royalists during the Civil War, and heavily in debt, in 1674 the Macleans found themselves under legal orders to surrender their lands and castle to the Campbells of Argyll. This was bitterly opposed, but by 1692 the Macleans were no longer in a position to carry out effective resistance and their possessions were given up. The castle was vacated, sometimes later used as a garrison, but ultimately became ruinous. In the late 19th century the Duke of Argyll sold a portion of the former Maclean lands, together with the castle, which came into the hands of Colonel Campbell of Possil, who re-sold it to A C Guthrie. In 1911 some of the past prestige of the Macleans was restored when the castle and some adjoining land was purchased from Murray Guthrie by Sir Fitzroy Maclean, 10th Baronet of Duart. In 1912 a world-wide reunion of Macleans was held at Duart to celebrate the restoration of the castle as the permanent residence of the Chief. Sir Fitzroy, a veteran of the Crimean War, lived to the age of 101 and was succeeded in 1936 by his grandson, Sir Fitzroy D Maclean, as the 27th Chief of the Clan.

The new Chief is an enthusiastic supporter of the Scout movement throughout the world, becoming Chief Scout, a post from which he retired in recent years on being elevated to the title of Lord Maclean and appointed Lord Chamberlain to the Royal Household. He is also Lord Lieutenant of Argyll.

The castle is open to the public daily in summer and attracts large numbers of visitors to view the varied objects of interest, the exhibition of Scouting, the massive construction of a typical Highland castle, and the views from the battlements. Refreshments and catering are available.

East of Duart the castellated tower near the point — best seen from the sea — is a memorial to William Black; one of his most stirring tales, *Macleod of Dare*, was located here.

The final attraction is in complete contrast to the antiquities of Duart. A mile and a half from Craignure we go in by a side road — well-signposted — through the policies and fine old timber to Torosay Castle, actually a handsome Victorian mansion designed in the Scottish Baronial Style by David Bryce in 1856. Here you will see records and portraits of the Guthrie family going back beyond the date when the house was first built, descriptions of more modern adventurous expeditions under sail and of incidents of the 1939-45 War, and many other items of interest. The house is open to the public, and conveniently situated as it is to Craignure, it attracts crowds of visitors. The gardens are a showplace, with the Statue Walk laid out by John Lorimer and the leafy paths along the little stream past the tall trunks of mature trees. Like Duart, there are excellent catering facilities here, very welcome after the walk along woodland roads from Craignure.

A feature which will be unique in the Hebrides and a major local attraction is the construction of a 10¼ inch narrow gauge railway from Craignure to the Castle. The road bed has been prepared, rails and rolling stock obtained, and it is hoped that by another season the trains will be rolling. If it proves a success it may be extended to Duart sometime in the future.

We have travelled together for many miles to explore the variety of interests in ancient Dalriada, Argyll and the Isle of Mull, and learned at first-hand something of their history and traditions, as well as present problems which are not all appreciated in the distant south. You have met a warm-hearted race of people whose heritage goes back into prehistory, but whose painful evolution was little understood by remote central Governments, leaving as a result a record of social injustices now long since forgiven, but not to be forgotten. You will remember the cloud shadows racing across the moorlands, the blue of the high mountains, the flash of a silvery fish in clear waters, and the unforgettable colours of a Hebridean sunset seen from the north of Mull late on a summer evening across the distant islands. Only the visitor who comes again and again can get to know this timeless land and its welcoming people.